The M
Who Spoke Chinese

A Family Memoir

Áine Downey

First published December 2019
Extended edition: December 2020
Colmcille Press
Ráth Mór
Bligh's Lane
Creggan, Derry
BT48 0LZ

ISBN 978 1 914009 02 0

Designed by Joe McAllister
Compiled and edited by Garbhán Downey & Cormac Downey
Copyright © Áine Downey/Colmcille Press

Cover photograph: The Morton family, Irish speakers from Belfast, celebrated in a newspaper clipping (late 1940s): back (l-r), Antoine, Diarmaid, Deirdre; front (l-r), Áine, Máire Róisín, Brigdín.

Back photograph: The Morton family in the Donegal Gaeltacht, c.1945: (l-r) Áine, Brigdín, Máire Róisín, Antoine, Diarmaid, Deirdre, Biddie Pheadar Mháire, and Risteard.

For Rónán
Le grá

Introduction to the First Edition*

Áine has spent her life writing letters. We have stacks of blue aerograms jam-packed with stories to the very last corner from her many travels – and just as many again sent by her when we were out on our own expeditions. Every time you pick up an old book, a card or letter falls out. Always when they're needed most. In recent times, Áine has even started writing letters to her grandchildren – at their insistence. Forget the phone, videophone and instant messaging: why shouldn't they get the same special treatment as their fathers?

Áine's letters are, for the most part, written to be shared; indeed, sometimes they actually necessitate group participation. When Áine was lecturing in India in the 1980s, she would chapterise her letters, sending single-sheet aerograms to each of us, with instructions as to who to contact next for the rest of the news.

More recently, partly at our behest and partly because she loves doing it, Áine has been writing us letters containing reminisces of her childhood, and they are quite inspiring. The Belfast, Donegal and occasionally Tyrone of her memories are living and breathing places; colourful, compassionate and kind. Often very funny and offbeat too. We meet a cat who uses a toilet, a whippet who believes a Labrador is his pet, a father who mortifies his children by singing on trams, and a recently-departed woman who comes back from the dead to get the priests to say a High Mass.

We may not have managed to compile a complete

collection here: there are stories Áine wrote for her surviving siblings, Diarmaid and Brigdín, or her sister Deirdre's daughters Gráinne, Dunla and Laoise (or, indeed, for her lifelong friends Nuala Morton and Fionnuala Geary) that we may well have missed. Thankfully, however, Áine does copy both of us into most of her correspondence, so we should have the bulk of it.

Just in case, however, we are calling this Volume One. That, and we want her to write more.

Cormac & Garbhán
December 2019

[*Áine had been working on the new edition of this book at the time of her death in May 2020. The additional material, along with some further biographical detail, is included in the second section of the book, 'In Continuum'.]

I

Biddie Pheadar Mháire,
Mrs Morton, Mammy, Neanaí

Frank Sinatra sings: 'When I was seventeen, it was a very good year', and I think of Biddie Pheadar Mháire at seventeen, who had been working in a sweet shop at the corner of Royal Avenue and the Donegall Street since the age of twelve. (Mammy always pointed to the same shop whenever I would pester her). It seems some older family members were working in Belfast and had lodgings on the Street and she would be looked after by them.

Rural barren Donegal couldn't, and didn't, treat its young girls with loving kindness; the immediate choice facing the twelve-year old was the hiring fair or some other form of paid employment by moving out to send money home. (Nuala thinks at some stage Biddie also worked in a fish shop.)

I know nothing about her social life in Belfast before being introduced to Richie. I have no idea how Biddie knew this bus driver Mister Ward: it seems that this bus driver who was familiar with Daddy and knew of his love of Irish, somehow knew Biddie Pheadar Mháire spoke Irish and introduced them.

In my imagination Biddie would have seen marrying a handsome, popular teacher as a route to financial security, and at the age of twenty-eight in St Patrick's Chapel on Donegall Street, on the feast of Sts Peter and Paul, Biddie became Mrs Morton.

The honeymoon was on Lough Derg, as was (seemingly) the tradition in Graffy. Biddie didn't return home except for funerals, she never spoke about her early life and, according to Auntie Ellie (married to her brother Peter/Peadar), their childhood wasn't easy and he would never go back to visit.

There is a story of the granny's funeral involving Uncle Neil/Niall in Glenties wearing the British Army uniform having a drink. However, I have been told another brother was also in uniform, so I am not sure if Neil's fall from grace was the uniform or the drink, or something entirely different, but the fall must have been fairly dramatic and traumatic as not one of the brothers or sisters came to his funeral. The only relative, besides myself was Johnny McHugh, the stationmaster in Glenties and brother-in-law: the McDermott memory goes long and deep.

Leaving aside that I was totally abandoned to bury the uncle I still remained in fairly close touch and I was to be found at McDermott funerals, with my back to many cupboard doors holding in skeletons; I was told nothing, the bones of the skeletons were all communicated by 'looks' and innuendos. While, through Neil, I got in touch with and wrote to Paddy in Glasgow and for a while Paul needed somewhere to stay in Derry, no mention was never ever made of the childhood growing up years, but there was definitely a big Glenties rift in later years involving a half-acre of bog.

Poverty has a lot to answer for.

* * *

Mrs Morton didn't have very many close friends, Breige an Easpaig, Sister Mary Francis – always with another nun (pre Vatican II, habit-wearing nuns travelled in pairs), Daddy and Mammy McCann and relatives; these are the memorable Mammy friends.

The McCann visits were significant and held in the privacy of the parlour – I see myself curled on the third step, at the bend in the stairs, listening to the records being played on the wind-up gramophone, especially Little Brigid Flynn, although my absolute favourite was Greensleeves with the Celtic Lament (the 78 records had a different melody on each side). I have since wondered if a tipple of Bristol Cream, the only alcohol I knew to touch the lips of women, might have been buried deep in Mammy McCann's handbag and that this contributed to the childhood memory of the happiness of their visits.

There were lots of Irish language acquaintances. Clara Street was an open house yet, as in the Martha-Mary parable, Mrs Morton was the Martha. It was good to creep under the kitchen table and listen to the conversations of these priests and teachers. In the main the food was griddle scones with an occasional exquisite apple tart, and so my remaining quietly under the table was sometimes rewarded with a piece.

I think it was through the teachers that Mrs Morton, who was a native speaker, was asked to adjudicate the Ashbourne Shield, a schools award for excellence and proficiency in spoken Irish. Outside of family funerals these were the only times I recall her getting time away (escaping) from us: time for and by herself and her work was remembered and much admired. Mrs Morton had all of two nights away from home, Derry and Enniskillen, I hope she cherished these occasions – we suffered Daddy's porridge, a to-be-remembered dish but not a to-be-repeated delicacy.

At a time when the lives of women were not exactly visible, never mind memorable, Mrs Morton's Ashbourne Shield reputation was remarkable.

* * *

I assume it was Daddy's decision to use Irish as the language of their home, certainly no other member of the McDermott family continued to use the native tongue in their adult life, in fact I always had the impression that Auntie Annie really disapproved of this misguided decision, yet Mammy always spoke Irish where and when possible.

A woman who was passionate about education, the 'three big ones' remember her bringing their reading books to bed, to make sure she was a few pages ahead, and both Máire Róisín and I were transported, via Gael Linn scholarship, to the Gaeltacht for a school year – Mammy regarded the National School system as far superior to the system in the North. I have no idea how Brigdín escaped.

Mammy was the great baker of tarts, pies, and scone bread, but her cabbage, turnip, and Senna-tea were not to my taste at all, at all.

A memory image of Mammy sitting in a comfortable chair in the warm kitchen, being able to close us out by wearing Diarmaid's home made crystal set over her ears, knitting each of her daughters Aran dresses (I think Gráinne F. still has Deirdre's) and the Aran wool double-moss-stitch coats, while we, willingly, did the cooking. Mammy seemed so content, not a worry in the world, this was multitasking at its best, crystal set blocking us out, listening to the radio, book on lap and not missing a stitch!

The Friday Saint George's market in Oxford Street was beside where Daddy taught; this was the source of fresh, good-value food where everyone knew and respected Mammy; here she was in her element. Conversations revolved around the usual family matters with the addition of passing on information on bargains. The one I remember best is Mammy being informed about when the 'seconds' of the good quality Irish linen for the latest ship would be available and what would Mammy like to be put aside for home use and/or gifts. And so from flour bags bleached and sewn together as bed sheets, we moved on to sleep on the best of linen. And, mind you, a surplus of bed linen was essential. Mammy really enjoyed the

Cumann Gaelach functions; it was mostly Deirdre's friends that seemed to come from the other Irish universities and this meant the sleeping arrangements of extra mattresses on bedroom floors, and under high beds – Mammy was in her element, everyone talking in Irish and herself central to the activity. (I do not have memories of Mammy with Diarmaid or Antoine's friends but that says more about me; their friends didn't spoil me the way Deirdre's did.)

But my favourite Mammy memory is Saturday nights in Clara Street. Fire lit, as always, furniture moved around to give the floor a good weekly scrum, the Irish News spread out drying the clean floor, we would sit ourselves (the three wee ones at least) around the hearth, turn off the radio with the red eye and Mammy would sing to us "Saol mór 'na chodladh, is mise liom fhéin". There was an intimacy in those occasions and you could sense her longing of barren Donegal in her voice, and being, when singing "muintir mo mhuintir".

* * *

Mammy had become Neanaí by the time Garbhán was born, and Deirdre brought her up to see him when he was three days old. Leaving aside the memories of Barley Sugar sweets, and that Rónán discovered by saying he wanted to be a priest was worth 50p, Neanaí still held tight to the need to please Auntie Annie.

As a widow she lived with Brigdín and Pat and

came visiting every so often here in Derry where she voluntarily helped in one of the local playgroups. Neanaí put the fear of God into me by stopping British/Scottish soldiers (most of the patrols here were Scottish regiments) and talking to them in Irish, insisting that she would understand Scottish Gaelic and if they didn't have any they were letting the side down. The dread when you spotted at a distance the tartan band on the beret and awaited the inevitable confused encounter, and I can assure you the determined McDermott streak was still alive, and I prepared my soul and awaited the inevitable.

In Neanaí's last weeks I have several image-memories: knowing this was the last journey, phoning home to tell Gerry where I had hidden the red transistor radio for Garbhán's birthday (I had already found it! – Ed.); Rónán, standing at the foot of her bed singing 'Deus Meus Adiuva Me'; Deirdre's kitchen, making enormous quantities of coleslaw and the temptation of the hanging spring-loaded decoration; the praying and the more praying and that we all knew the McDermott determination would wait until we were all there, (her image of a happy death) but especially that Neanaí remembered the co-op discount number.

Le grá.

II

How to get a High Mass in Baile na Finne

There is a Morton-McDermott story involving the Second World War, evacuation from Belfast, moving from the relative comfort of Ravenhill Avenue to the shores of Loch Finn. Magnificent, romantic Ireland with the backdrop of the Blue Stack mountains and, most important, a National School, but not yet benefitting from the electricity, running water and modern facilities of 1940s Belfast.

Poor Biddie Pheadar Mháire, on her own, with five children and expecting me: having to draw the water from the well and trying to light the big open hearth-grate with the damp Blue Stack mountainy turf – in order to heat the water, cook the food, keep the house warm, wash, and dry the clothes.

Those big open hearths were hard work: large iron bracket with horizontal iron pole and metal hook-chains for the big black kettle, the griddle, cauldrons and 'Dutch oven' for baking; every aspect of the fireplace and hearth being utilised.

Life wasn't exactly a bed of roses for Daddy either; teaching in Oxford Street, living in the Braniel, having unsuccessful eye surgery (the cataract was successfully removed, however, you had to keep your head absolutely still for three weeks but the Blitz had other plans and so he lost the sight in the eye), and missing us.

Here in Baile na Finne, we were unknowingly being introduced to a woman who would be very influential in my life, a woman who was dead maybe two years before I was born, a woman without a name of her own.

The only house in the Glenties locality for the Morton family was 'Sean Teach Phat Kelly' and, as Pat Kelly's old house, it really was a barn.

When Daddy came to Fintown for the school holidays, it was his initial visit to this area of Donegal. The first morning, he rose early and away out with him in search of mushrooms for the breakfast.

He noticed an old woman hunker-sitting near the stone wall at the bottom of the hill.

He didn't speak to her on his way out, but she was still there and him returning, so he thought perhaps he would practice his Irish. This thought had just entered his mind when the old woman moved very quickly up the hill away from him. Because Daddy didn't know the-lie-of-the-land, and with his eyesight, not being great he didn't follow her.

Later that first day, Mammy and himself went off to drop in on the neighbours, and Daddy asked them about the sprightly old woman. He recounted all that had occurred, and off they all went to inspect the place. Bean Pat Kelly, and her dead a year or more, she was the person who sat at that very spot, ag buachailleacht bó (tending the cows).

Naturally, Daddy was alarmed by this and sufficiently anxious as to consult the priest. There he learned that she had left £100; (one hundred pounds – how on earth did this bean gan ainm manage to scrimp and save such an enormous amount of money!) This money was for a High Mass to be said for the repose of her soul. But with a war being on and the necessity to have three priests to say a High Mass, and the problem of food for a meal, the Mass had not been read. I was told the High Mass was read before the month was out.

* * *

I now realise the influence of this bean gan ainm (woman without a name) towards the Morton qualities of determination, perseverance, persistence, getting value for money and not letting anybody put one over on you. Míle buíochas, Bean Pat Kelly.

III

Maiden aunts

Life is easy to chronicle, but bewildering to practice.
(EM Forster)

Growing up in Belfast in the immediate postwar period every family had the support of a legion of maiden aunts. In our case Daddy's sisters, Florrie and Josie.

I never really wondered about the 'why' of this until 1979/1980 when Rónán was acting in My Dear Palestrina along with JG Devlin.

Now, it so happened that it was Daddy and JG, as young men, who founded the Cluain Árd in Belfast, and so Richie Morton's grandson was taken under JG's wing. This proud Belfast man, on the first of July, sat Rónán down and told him the horror story, on this the anniversary of the massacre of a generation of young Belfast men at the Battle of the Somme. While he was talking, it was only then I realised that one of the 'never talked about' consequences of this First World War Battle was the leaving behind of a generation of all these beautiful young women, who brightened and contributed so much up our fairly drab lives and became known as 'maiden aunts'.

The Eleven-Plus Education Act of the 1940s ensured that the Morton family returned from Baile na Finne for Deirdre to sit the examination for the continuation of education at a grammar school. I think it might have been called the City/Corporation Scholarship in the early days (but Diarmaid or Brigdín will check my memory).

It was the Clara Street address that Deirdre had to use for the examination (the Braniel was about a mile outside the city boundary), and I kind of assume we were legally in residence there for Diarmaid's turn. While I am unsure of whether or not the joint 'Queens of the May' photograph of Deirdre and Nellie Agnew was before 1942, or the year of the return, with both dressed in their white multipurpose dresses and 'pearl' tiaras leading the procession, carrying a statue of Our Lady, around the school yard – I assume it was pre-evacuation? This is the same Nellie who sent the doll with the china face to Florrie all the way from America to help Santa locate my gift. Maiden aunts recognised the importance of staying in touch.

In addition, the NHS was in the early stage of development and it was the paper prescription medication, one payment for all the medication on the list, and so the child Áine was sent to Dr Hunter's surgery with a list of requirements. However, the Mrs Cullen's headache powders were additional to these, yet absolutely essential for Daddy's headaches and therefore harmony in the home.

Being poor (and I didn't have any idea that we were when I was growing up) was the way of life for everyone, yet in hindsight I feel sorry for Mammy who having married a teacher, must have had the expectation that she wouldn't have to scrimp and then scrimp some more. However, Daddy didn't (on principle) take the oath of allegiance to the English king and so his pay was minimal as a teacher in the Christian Brothers Oxford Street primary school.

Daddy did make up for the extravagance of Mrs Cullen though, by honing a seven o'clock razor blade on a glass tumbler so that one blade lasted the week.

* * *

When we evacuated to Donegal during the war, he stayed with Florrie and Josie, his sisters, our maiden aunts, at in the Braniel (at some stage Máire Róisín also stayed), and when we returned with the extra Áine from Donegal, I am led to believe we all stayed with them until Daddy Kelly came up with the house-key for 3 Clara Street. Diarmaid has the story of him buying a bun in Curry's with his saved bus fare on the way home from school to mark my first birthday.

Florrie and Josie lived in one half of a semidetached house located in the middle of a field, the other half was occupied by a maiden aunt of the Agnews and I always assumed the house belonged to them. There was a magnificent lilac tree at the garden gate and, in a proper gypsy caravan unofficially located 'up the lane', lived Mr and Mrs Harris. I loved that caravan and, in my imagination, travelled freely around Ireland especially when it became permanently located in the Braniel garden.

The openness and generosity of these maiden aunts was renowned – Florrie when at Mass in Saint Matthew's noticed this mother and daughter carrying brown, well battered, suitcases; naturally she got into conversation with them only to discover that they were homeless, and so the Braniel became home to Blanche and Mrs Harkin, and while we benefited from the luxury of home made shortbread, the Harkin extended family benefited from two additional maiden aunts.

The only memory I have of Josie 'out' of the Braniel is the first New Year's Day when we moved to South Parade and bought a new parlour carpet with the Co-Op dividend money, (81861). Diarmaid, back from Bahrain, had the blue Ford Anglia with the Armagh LZ registration. I can see him lifting Josie out of the car to a chair on the left of the fire in the newly-carpeted parlour and thinking that this was such a special day.

And special days, special treats, wee surprises: for my generation of big families reared in the time of rationing and poverty, these were provided by our maiden aunts, a special race of forgotten women.

Le grá.

IV

The Mickeys who speak Chinese

Number 3 Clara Street, a house with big back/side yard and even a 'garden'. Okay, the dump, now a recycling unit, was behind that! The only house on that side of the street, alongside the park, more about the park later. Now with a 'Morton' plaque (courtesy of the Gaelic Tour of East Belfast), which I have yet to see.

Early childhood was/is simply a time for experiencing, you don't analyse and so I assumed everyone else's was the same as ours. Okay, I realised I was, for better and worse, the youngest of a family of eight, and six children was not a particularly large number; I probably assumed that every home had three bedrooms, one for the girls, a second for boys, and a mammy and daddy bedroom.

I did not, a child doesn't, distinguish between languages – so there was the family way of talking, spoken between and by us whether in the house or outdoors and normally spoken with the many visitors to 3 Clara Street. I didn't realise that this was 'Irish' and was different from the way of communicating at St Anthony's Primary School and outside playing in the street or in the park; seemingly that was called 'English'. I did not know, why would /should I know, that these were two different languages with different political preferences, different ideologies, you name it and these were different.

I do have a "Diarmaid brother memory" which I did not understand at the time and probably would not recall but it became a part of the Morton folklore and as I grew older it impacted on me. Diarmaid was at the adolescent age of 'badges on the jacket lapels', a pioneer pin and a gold fáinne. The double identity of Catholic and Irish speaking. It seems when he got off the bus for our street he would put up the jacket collar, thereby turning in the lapel badges. He realised the secrets were out when he was approached with the polite query: "Are you the Mickeys who speak Chinese?" The implications of all this didn't impact on the five-year-old Áine; utterly and completely meaningless it was.

* * *

It must have been when education-through-Irish was impacting in a disconcerting way on the Belfast psyche/consciousness, and I may have been involved in Comhairle na Gaelscolaíochta, that the baggage-significance of this 'bilingualism' hit home many years later. Sunday Sequence asked me to be part of a panel discussion on the Irish language; naturally when I arrived at the studio in Belfast my first question was whether the discussion was to be conducted in Irish or English. My question was greeted by shock, slight hysteria, but not derision. However 'their' first question was how different did I feel being reared in both Irish and English; my response, which was the absolute truth, was that I assumed everyone was, why should I think otherwise.

End of their anticipated discussion to turn me into some kind of oddity, if not freak, as I was not going there.

V

Clara Park

Deep is your longing for the land of your memories.
(Kahlil Gibran, The Prophet)

A sheet of corrugated iron separated our house from the entry lane leading to the Belfast dump. The park was on the other side of the entry and, to go to play there, we went out the brown serrated-brown painted front door (what do you call that way of painting the door?) and skipped or Irish-danced the few hundred yards to the official gate.

Those corrugated iron sheets were renowned for their durability. However, these were the days of sweetie rationing and sharing was the order of the day. So, with great childhood persistence and tools of small stones and specifically the tool for taking stones out of horses hooves from a 'borrowed' Swiss Army penknife we carved an eye-level hole just big enough to pass through a bulls-eye, a piece of chewed chewing gum, or, better still, bubble gum. I am wondering now if these gifts were signs of childhood affection because I have no memory of us ever having a spare sweet, and chewing gum was a definite no-no.

Miss Green wasn't married to the park keeper Mr Jack with the limp, except in my imagination, and the pair of them looked after the physical place, locked up the swings, and organised various events, especially the children's concert party for the 1953 Coronation.

There was a multipurpose, fairly large hut for sheltering /protecting Miss Green and Mr Jack and for us children to practice our prowess on rainy days. The main hut-day, keep-fit activities involved throwing bean bags and learning steps for Scottish dancing, not really Morton-type events, but kept us safe, dry and out of the house.

Clara Park was, like all the Northern Ireland parks (and most activities) subject to the Sunday Observance local legislation – poor insecure God needing to ensure that there were no distractions to stop children going 'voluntarily' to the churches, the Sunday schools, and the gospel halls. And so, the swings, swing-boats, roundabout, slides were ensconced in thick steel chains – not even the Swiss army penknife could scratch, never mind sever, a link in those chains.

The tarmacadam surface impacted, though I didn't realise it at the time; as far as I was concerned if you fell on that tarmacadam surface you got hurt, scratched, bled and Miss Green cleaned up the injury and you learned to be more careful. I do recall Máire Róisín having a broken arm and assuming this was due to a fall off a swing-boat. Brigdín was positively acrobatic on the swings and my favourite was playing with two balls or, better still, three – I would play/ practice different tricks for hours on the park shed wall and inside this shed if it was raining. The wooden shed's inside surface was artistically adorned by all of our initials, using one of the many extremely useful

25

gadgets of the Swiss army penknife.

The tarmacadam surface must have jarred with me. Through this I started to notice the significance of different surfaces; rich people up the Castlereagh Road, had a wee green grass garden, poor people had yards. Rich people's streets had trees as well as lampposts distributing bright electric light; poor people's streets did not have trees; however, our outdated gas lampposts, individually lit at dusk, were absolutely perfect for the rope swinging when parks were closed.

* * *

It seems the 1953 Coronation was a huge event for the citizens of the area. In the days without/before television, local concerts were a familiar entertainment and I certainly wasn't aware that we were putting on anything special. Us three wee Mortons were quick learners, another way of expressing that we loved to show off. So we would be on stage for most of the show and this was going to be quite a long concert, with individual and choral singing, a Scottish sword dance and the usual individual recitations.

Just as we were preparing to mount the stage Miss Green turns to the three of us and sends us home to get cups! By the time we returned every other child had received a Coronation Mug and the English national anthem had been sung and applauded.

In later years, I realised this had been prearranged with the parents as the condition for us participating but at the time I did mind not getting a new mug.

VI

Mary Foster visits Clara Street

Where did she sleep? Was this one of the many times that the three wee ones shared the single bed by the window overlooking the back yard (if you stood up on tip-toes on the bed you could just about see who was out playing in the park across the entry), two at the top with the feet of the third. However, there was the comfortable, slightly claustrophobic, alternative to put one of the many, heaped 'discarded' mattresses from the big bed underneath on the floor, and one or more of us three wee ones would sleep there. Either way, I assume Mary Foster slept with Deirdre in the double bed, which, with the single bed, more or less filled the room.

She was always called Mary Foster, never Mary, and somehow she lived permanently with, and was part of, the McGrath's. With child-like logic, I assumed that the 'foster' meant she was fostered, and my child-eyes saw that it was she who did the housework and kept the big farmhouse in a suitable condition for such a highly-regarded family.

That double bed always reminded me of 'The Princess and the Pea' and naturally when I had the opportunity to sleep in it, I was convinced I really was a princess.

However, sleep arrangements were just the tip of

the iceberg of mini-considerations. In the knowledge that all would be reported back to Auntie Annie, my mother's sister, the house was cleaned, spotless it was, for her visit. The McGrath's lived in Killen, Coalisland, County Tyrone; they were by the standards of the time wealthy and holidayed in Portstewart (not Donegal); this being the seaside for the upwardly mobile northern Catholics. The Catholic upward mobility was comparable to the Indian caste system, not totally based on wealth but also on 'position' in society and, in the Clara Street days, they had not one but two 'ábhar sagartan' in the family. Naturally, we were a bit of a disappointment to our mother, not a potential nun or priest among us.

My main fascination with Mary Foster's visit was the unpacking of the big, spotlessly-clean, glass sweet jar in which she kept not only her most prized possessions but the most envied possessions of all the young women in those late 1940s, clothes-rationed times; delicate, possibly American, definitely smuggled, black market, fine (oh, so fine) nylon stockings. Nylon stockings with the black line up the back, not a stitched ladder in sight, such was the care taken of these precious possessions, hence the glass jar for their protection. Not only did I not touch the stockings, but I didn't even dare touch the glass jar.

However particular Mary Foster was about her precious nylons, her washing lettuce was a work of art. All the lettuce in those olden days was properly garden grown and a source of nutrition for the natural, soil-based bugs; nowadays (with our obsession for cleanliness) an endangered species.

It was the greenfly that was the most prolific and easily missed, except by the expert; each leaf was held up to the light and every piece of evidence of their existence was eliminated. I always thought of a Mary Foster salad as 'high tea'; her trying to introduce us to the ways in which the Catholic elite lived, aspirations with a kind of pretentiousness, and yet we really liked her and her coming for a night or two on the GNR train to visit was a treat for her too.

Living, as we do now, in a time wherein we seek living legacies, well look no further – the assumed tradition of fostering goes deep and is why the Irish-speaking Scruffy, Fiachra and Brónagh's very-nearly Labrador, is living with me in long-term foster care. Just as particular as Mary Foster when it comes to where to sleep and, especially, the purity of his dog food.

VII

A most mannerly cat

Pangur Breac was a mouser. This was, presumably, a prerequisite for a cat whose primary reason for being with us was to ensure an absence of vermin in the bottles of alcohol sold in the shops supplied from this bottling yard. We rented the house from Daddy Kelly who owned an off-licence at the corner of Clara Street and the Beersbridge Road in Belfast. The delivery lorry was parked in this yard, our back yard, where the Guinness and beer were dispensed into the stone bottles and then delivered to various establishments: so in a sense Pangur was my introduction to health and safety concerns in the food and drink industry.

It wasn't that Pangur wasn't a house cat; it was more that he was a 'place' cat; unlike Pangur Bán who assisted the monks transcribe the Book of Kells and was definitely a people cat. Additionally, our Pangur was totally independent; the bottling yard was his primary source of nutrition and, additionally, our wee house backing, as it was, onto the city dump was kept totally mouse free.

Given that there would be men working in the yard, there was a proper flush toilet in the yard. Mind you, given that I have no memory of a wash-hand basin I'm not so sure about the effectiveness of any health and safety legislation.

Now, all the houses in the street had outside toilets; ours was the only one with an indoor toilet but given that there were eight of us in the family there were times when the outside one was necessary. Antoine it was on this particular occasion who lifted the latch, opened the door and there was independent Pangur sitting on the wooden seat tending to his ablutions. Well, being from a mannerly family, Antoine says, "Och, gabh mo leithscéal, 'brón orm, Pangur," and, naturally, closes the door after himself.

There was always reading material in the toilet. In our case it was the extremely, multi-useful, daily Irish News. Firstly the ordinary, two pages of death notices, accompanied by a family history running commentary, the Belfast equivalent of Derry's "Which Doherty would that be?" Next came the funeral reports and the issue of upward or downward in the Irish caste system; the number and seniority of the priests attending the funeral carefully counted, commented, compared and decisions in relation to the significance of the family determined.

I have no memory of the actual news giving rise to such intense scrutiny and, as far as I was concerned, news coverage could be read later. When the paper was discarded by the adults, three or four paper sticks for lighting tomorrow's fire were created; the rest of the sheets folded into at least eight and with a sharpish knife sliced, a knitting needle hole pierced the left hand corner, threaded with a piece of discarded cord and attached to the nail in the toilet, for reading the news prior to the final use. Recycling in the 1940s and 1950s lived and died with the multipurpose Irish News. Obviously, in other people's toilets you encountered different papers consequently. As well as contrasting the different editorial news coverage, the quality of the paper was also the subject of much important discussion.

In my eyes there was a hierarchy of toilets, we had an indoor one as had the Braniel, and, naturally, Auntie Annie's had two indoor toilets, one for upstairs and one downstairs, but it was the outside ones that I found particularly fascinating/interesting.

VIII

The third Sunday of the month

Mammy made great pastry, known the length and breadth of Ireland, using a marble slab to roll out the dough with a milk bottle. Later, AN Other must have procured a rolling pin for Mrs Morton; I have tried the marble and bottle approach, I now know it was her light touch and I have resorted to the shop-bought variety. (With apologies to Brigdín and Nuala, the next best pastry maker to Mammy is Fionnuala Geary.)

Meat was still rationed yet there was a butcher on the Falls Road, miles away from Clara Street (near where Daddy and Mammy McCann lived). So the Saturday before the third Sunday of the month would find the 6/7/8-year old Áine walking up the Falls Road to, what I now realise was in those days of rationing, the black market butcher for "a pound and a half of stewing steak and a pound of sausages". (I say a pound and a half, simply because the Friday fish message was "a pound and a half of the thin end of the white fish".)

That Saturday the pastry was made with the non-rationed (Echo) margarine and both the meat pie and the apple tart baked. The hair wash was followed by the weekly performance of the painful putting in the ringlets, hair brushed around cloth rags, how I hated that procedure and inevitably a few hairs would be tightly caught in the rags (did God really count the hairs on my head!), so sleep was fraught.

Comhlacht Mhuire was at three-o'clock on the third Sunday of the month in St Mary's Chapel in the town centre, however, the ringlets had to be 'refreshed' with a hot poker in order to be respectful of the Morton reputation and to make God pleased with us. In my memory it was by tram we travelled, it could have been a trolley bus but for some reason my memory is a tram.

I dreaded if we had to stand for the journey because as soon as Daddy got the hold of the steadying strap he would start singing: "Do not forsake me oh my darling…"; that was simply embarrassing. And as if that wasn't bad enough, the amount of the bus fares was never a normal transaction, always had to be a mathematical puzzle …like 2 to the power of 17 divided by 3 squared….

As a youngster, the journey home was even more excruciating as by then we all had the extra need to go to the toilet. (Antoine's story of Pangur is documented already.)

And now, having prayed with the few other Gaelic-speaking families and reached home, came the big tea. Father McGuckian, with Margaret Thompson, came about six in the evening, as did the last-remaining piece of the carefully-hidden, saved butter ration. Antoine was extremely effective /efficient at finding our mother's hiding places, but to no avail on the third week of the month. I cannot emphasise strongly enough how the butter ration was cherished, only to have it was produced for the table on the third Sunday tea.

* * *

I still haven't forgiven the priest: seventy years later, I can still see him putting the knife into the precious, rationed butter, getting a BIG knob and placing it in a totally unconcerned manner on the warm pastry of the world's best apple tart. All I could think of was another week of the dreaded, dark-yellow slab margarine.

IX

My first silver sixpence

Putting the dog-food-knife in its special separate place in the cutlery drawer this memory surfaced.

It was still in the pre Vatican II days when not a drop of water could touch the tongue, not even a tooth-cleaning drop, from midnight Saturday until after communion at the 9.00am Sunday Mass at Saint Anthony's, Willowfield.

After the Senna-tea Saturday morning breakfast, keeping constipation at bay, the Sunday preparation began. However, the Senna-tea experience merits a sentence or two in its own right as it is also my first memory (?) of the usefulness of being open to bribery.

Keeping healthy was a government requirement, liquid cod liver oil was distributed regularly by the school nurse, as were big bottles of "orange juice", (the colour was correct, the taste questionable). Our home had a special smelly cod liver oil spoon, kept separately in the cutlery drawer and, after the morning hair plaiting experience, we formed a queue for this daily health-giving concoction. Being the youngest I was the last in the line and the gross, smelly, nauseous anticipation was never to be forgotten; absolutely disgusting. In addition, most homes bought "malt" for special occasions as well as the dreaded Senna tea for the weekly detox.

I have no memory of Diarmaid or Antoine participating in this Saturday morning ritual, but I recall that it was Deirdre who bribed me for a silver sixpence to throw up and put an end to this particular horror. A silver, sixpenny-piece all for myself, and I knew the adventure I could now explore.

* * *

The Sunday preparation ritual could now begin with one of us wee ones (usually myself) being dispatched to Gilroy's shop, Ann Street, Belfast, to buy the pound and a half of pork sausages for the special, post-communion fry. By dispatched I mean sent, with exactly the correct money, to walk down the town. Hail, rain or snow, yet despite any discomfort the freedom of this escape from the Saturday morning house-cleaning, a potential visit to Littlewoods if there were sufficient funds for six slices of middle-cut bacon and this week, thanks to the bribe, a Woolworths record counter visit to enquire about the latest Jo Stafford hit. Such a Saturday adventure.

Having the silver sixpence in my pocket gave me the confidence to approach and speak to the sophisticated salesgirl. In retrospect, my lack of sophistication and total ignorance must have been obvious, but that Saturday morning, as far as I was concerned, this eight-year-old was in total control of the situation. Oh yes, we had the wind-up gramophone so I knew how to hold the Jo Stafford 78 record properly and, on realising the cost of the precious fragile disc, I looked the sales assistant in the eye and said I was looking for a record of Jo singing solo without the background orchestra, and I walked away with my head held high, fingering the small silver sixpence in my pocket.

Le grá.

X

Born to dance

Men and boys whistled in the streets, young girls linked arms and sang in harmony, and us 1940s' babies practiced our dance steps while walking to school: a h-aon, dó, trí, 's a h'aon, dó, trí; kicking our skinny wee legs high in the air to the Irish dance steps. It was from Anne Jennings, who had aspirations to be an Irish dancer, that I copied/learned the more complicated moves, the heel rock and the difference between a jig and a reel.

There was a clear demarcation line between Irish dancing and Scottish dancing in Clara Street: Irish in the street, and Scottish in the park hut; my introduction to red lines. It was Miss Green who, on wet days when we were confined to the hut, would take out the wooden sticks, lay them out on the floor as crossed swords and as with 'musical chairs' the race was on to get the right toe pointing at the head of a sword.

I have no memory of the music we attempted to dance to, but as Scottish dancing was to be performed at wee park concerts we rote-learned the steps and us three wee ones were willing to please and simply loved to dance.

Ducky Mallon was the céilí dance teacher in Ranafast – and about the ages of six or seven (Daddy was teaching in the Irish College), we had Teach

Owen Dhonaghaí Owenín, so I snuck into the back of the afternoon class and was introduced to the 'burl'. Given a choice between refined, mannerly Scottish dancing or the rampant freedom of the burl – you can work out for yourself which I choose. Suffice to say I was hooked, especially by a Sean Lavery burl.

* * *

The weather had a second significant part to play in the learning to dance. At St Dominic's on wet lunchtimes, we were all ushered into the Assembly Hall where a nun, usually Sister Philippa, lined us up and taught us The Gay Gordons, the Military Two-Step and The Polka (presumably to get rid of surplus energy). Occasionally, an old-time waltz or foxtrot might be included. It wasn't just Irish literature that this order of nuns ignored – the music song and dance heritage was another major area that was not to be encouraged. This learning of British (perceived as sophisticated) dances was to be encouraged...

I was always tall for my age so when it came to assigning the gender position to learn to dance, I was always the male and the man took the lead in ballroom dancing and especially the jive – not the most forward thinking idea to bridge the gap between dancing at school and Fruithill or the Plaza dancehalls; for that genetic height gene I could have, at any Belfast dancehall, been identifiable as not only Catholic but also Dominican-educated.

Antoine, however, had years earlier unwittingly rescued me from that fate. He was at the 'romantic' stage of development, going around the house singing 'Goodnight Irene', learning to ballroom dance using the John Dosser School of Dancing patterns and needed a partner to practice. At the age of eight or nine, I was to be found in the kitchen of Clara Street with the appropriate pattern laid out on the floor and the wind-up gramophone playing Greensleeves or The Celtic Lament in Antoine's arms learning to be a female ballroom dancer.

Antoine teaching me to dance by 'pattern' served me in good stead during my ballroom dancing days – in the first place the girl had to be asked to dance (except there was always one 'ladies choice' and one Paul Jones), and frequently the rhythm-less man asked what the actual dance was: the problem was that, regardless of the music, the man started the John Dosser step-pattern immediately on receiving the information: I never thanked Antoine for teaching me how to dance all these steps regardless of the rhythm/tempo of the music.

Despite all these attempts to teach me non-Irish dancing, it was still the h-aon, dó, trí that remained the dance of choice, and the summer that Brigdín and I hitchhiked around Ireland and learned the 'Kerry Set' remains the highlight of the dancing years.

Through my dancing experiences, I always knew the answer to the 'inheritance versus the environment' question.

Le grá.

XI

'Handmades' and hand-me-downs

Every house had the sack of flour in the dry corner of the scullery. In the days before we needed 'recycling' and cloth was rationed, redundant flour sacks, the size of 20 kg coal bags nowadays, multitasked as bed linen – pillow cases, bolster cases and, with seams carefully unstitched and two bags sewn back together, you had bed sheets.

Somehow, the Morton family with four daughters had procured one, yes, the one, white, probably satin, multipurpose-adjustable length, dress. I always assumed it was, magically, Auntie Florrie-made rather than shop bought. The only photograph I ever saw of this dress was Deirdre and Nellie Agnew dressed in white, celebrating being the Queens of the May with the girls of Saint Anthony's School, Willowfield. They were joint Queens leading the prayerful procession, with statue, around the schoolyard. This dress adorned each of the four of us for First Communion, Confirmation and various religious occasions and special events.

The main memory I have of First Communion is the fear of the host sticking to the roof of my mouth. Under no circumstances was any non-priest permitted to touch the precious host; this would be absolute sacrilege and the nuns' watchful eyes would spot any finger/hand deviation from the prayerful joining of the hands at any stage of the, carefully-, even frequently-rehearsed sacramental act.

In the same year I made my Confirmation in St Matthew's Ballymacarett; for some Canon Law reason, it was beneath the Bishop's dignity to give this sacrament in St Anthony's (which was a 'chapel of ease'). My awesome, mouthwatering memory of Confirmation was on returning home and, still wearing the communal white dress, I made myself a scallion sandwich. I can still see and smell the juicy white bulb head of that scallion.

I never thought of the white dress as a hand-me-down, more a communal special that was passed along and, as I was the youngest, I was quite possibly permitted to 'wear it out' as a 'good' summer dress.

Real hand-me-downs were a different story; Deirdre was that wee bit older so her clothes were put aside for a few years, whereas I could watch Máire Róisín grow out of her coats, then Brigdín having her turn and, finally, the coat would be all mine.

There was one particular brown with white-flex tweed coat, with a brown velvet collar, that I eyed longingly while awaiting my turn. It was only shop-bought clothes that became the hand-me-downs; our mother's beautiful, hand-knitted garments were unappreciated. Everybody had hand knits.

Yet, in those days of clothes rationing there seemed to be no shortage of wool. The wool didn't come in balls, ready for the needles, it came in skeins, loosely coiled lengths that were held on outstretched hands (about shoulder width) and Mammy, or a trusted older sister, rolled the balls of wool (a tortuous, painful, keeping-still task for the skein holder). Such complicated knitting stitches, not simply the knit and purl but the cable, moss, double moss stitches and many more, and then the complicated knitting patterns, the women excelled in clothing us. We were fortunate in that Mammy loved knitting and really shone in the art. (Had Mammy not come to work in Belfast at the age of twelve, she could well have been one of the generation of Glenties women Aran knitters Patrick MacGill wrote about in The Rat Pit).

Diarmaid, and him only a potential engineer, had constructed two crystal sets, so, before we had the red-eyed radio, Mammy commandeered one set all to herself, blocked out our childish fighting and general noise and, wearing the big cuffed headphones, the needles never stopped, while she listened to the McCooeys or whatever the radio had to offer – bliss, peace.

* * *

The first shop bought clothes all for myself, the occasion is etched powerfully in the memory. Auntie Annie had access to a wholesale shop in May Street, Belfast for stocking their shop in Killen and Mammy had a McGrath Shop letterhead giving her permission to use the facility.

The occasion was the Children's Day at the Oireachtas in the Mansion House, Dublin and I was selected/volunteered to undertake the speech of gratitude on behalf of the children from the North (Buíochas ó Pháistí na Sé gCondaí). It was mostly for shoes the letterhead was produced, however, on this important occasion for the Morton family, I was going to be 'shop bought' clothed for the event. Daddy had written the speech, I learned it off by heart and practiced in front of every mirror in the house and every shop window I passed.

I didn't have any choice in the clothes. It never occurred to me to express any opinion, anyway I was overawed by the fact that clothes were being shop bought just for me. Wearing a brand new Fair Isle jumper and grey pleated skirt with braces, this magnificent eight-year-old, so proud to be standing on the stage in front of Bean de Valera and all of these important people (as far as I was concerned the whole world was there), performing Daddy's Irish speech, wearing brand new, shop-bought clothes.

* * *

We no longer have hand-me-downs we have charity shops or, for the nearly worn out items, recycling centres. However, thank God we still have some mothers who knit. The biggest change is in our appreciation of home/hand knits, acknowledging, at long last, the absolute beauty of these creations.

A friend's mother both knows the stories of the different traditional Aran stitches and is skilled in the art of their knitting. I now am the proud possessor and exhibitor of two, yes two, Duffy-Aran works of art: a mustard wool for autumn to winter, and a raspberry creation for special occasions and winter-spring. These magnificent, living, works of art will never be hand-me-downs; one will be part of my inheritance to granddaughter and the second one might be inherited by the more appreciative daughter-in-law.

In the meantime I am indulging in becoming familiar with the praise being heaped upon their beauty, and although I say 'this is a Duffy-Aran original', I become again the eight-year-old standing centre stage with the whole world looking admiringly at me.

Le grá.

XII

My hair, my rules?

The first memory I have that the hair on my head was not up to expectations is of the weekend ritual.

It starts on the Saturday evening with my mother carefully twisting clean wet clumps of three-year old hair around long uneven cloth rags/ threads: followed by a night of manfully (female-childfully) trying to find a comfortable way of settling on the pillow; the agony of the unwinding on Sunday morning, stray hairs tangled in the twists and cotton knots, unsuccessfully resisting being torn from my scalp; to produce for the congregation of the nine o'clock Mass in St. Anthony's Willowfield – or even for God – ringlets. Now for three weekends out of four, that was the end of the affair, however, on the third Sunday of the month we went to the Irish-language confraternity at three o'clock in the afternoon, and the fact that this hair of mine did not 'hold' the ringlets, the anticipated/regulatory eight hours led to a lifelong fear and hatred of red hot pokers.

Slightly later in life, I learned to dread the sight of the shiny steel, fine-tooth comb; this entails scalp-scraping of an intensity that makes chilblains-pain, or raw, scuffed-inside-of-knees-pain, seem very bearable, even pleasant. The sense of shame when nits were found at home was certainly preferable to the 'letting down the family name' disgrace when the nits were discovered by the school nurse.

* * *

Were the plaits really fine, easy, less painful? There were variations on the theme, depending on the fashion of the time: 'simple' middle parting and one or two plaits down the back. No, nothing simple about the middle parting; getting the parting exactly in the middle meant remaining absolutely still, not exactly a childhood trait and, as the fourth daughter in the line, I rapidly learned how to breathe without moving a muscle. The excruciating pain of a hair being caught on the wrong side of a plait – with plaits, the hair in question hadn't the wit to leave the scalp and consequently remained all day caught in an agonising taut grip.

The two plaits over the ears meeting at the crown of the head stretched such hairs to a pain that the wallowing in agony of ancient saints whose knotted belts and scapulars I wore next to the skin seemed totally incomprehensible – did they not have hair experiences like mine? How did they have to seek out, and subject themselves to, imposed bodily pain?

By adolescence, this hair on my head had, more or less, taken over my life except for the worry that the eyebrows, which were expanding, might meet in the middle. Daddy liked long hair so it wasn't until he went blind that I allowed Sylvester Maguire (the hairdresser on Ormeau Road) to cut it.

I ironed this hair to make it straight; I backcombed

the hair into a beehive when that was the fashion; this hair has been subjected to the 'afro' perm and being bleached blonde. It has been willed into the submission of flicks, streaks, anything but grey; and the amazing part is that it didn't fall out. Throughout adolescence, adulthood, the middle and later years, I thought that someone-else-out-there knew more about my hair that I did.

* * *

Eventually I got fed up with being told that this hair of mine is 'very fine' and that did not mean 'fine' as in pure gold, but 'fine' as in 'you don't expect that anyone can do anything with this'.

Alice Walker has a short story, "Oppressed Hair Puts A Ceiling On Your Brain", and eventually I realised this to be true. So, without receiving authority from any of the people who knew better, I disposed of the bleached blond clumps, I looked me in the eye and took control.

* * *

Pink goes well with grey, everyone knows that, and sure now even Helen Mirren has followed in my footsteps!

Dear God, I sincerely hope you have better things to do than worry about, never mind try to count, the hairs on my head.

Le grá.

XIII

Religious observances

The seeds of suspicion of both the Church and State were planted in the first month of my life, thanks to neither institution acknowledging my mother's chosen name for me as appropriate.

The constraints of both institutions dominated childhood. Postwar state-rationing – meat, butter, clothes, sugar, even sweets – ensured physical needs were, understandably, restricted; a temporary measure.

However, the Church's soul restrictions were much more restrictive and permanent, not only in this life but also the afterlife; Ten Commandments, Six Precepts of the Church, Seven Deadly Sins, Seven Sacraments (with the peril of Limbo for the un-baptised), Papal infallibility, mortal and venial sins, Canon laws, purgatory or hell; with the only possible relief being confession and indulgences.

Consequently, the specially-authorised prayers, on the feast of All Souls, were deeply ingrained in the child-psyche as the only way for dead relatives to escape from purgatory. And it was a rescue that was required: the fires of hell were for eternity, whereas escape was possible from the unspecified torture of purgatory.

For as far back as I can remember, I prayed, (among a long list of people) for my mother's brother Neil/Niall, with November 2nd as the day to rescue these souls from their torment. Six 'Our Fathers', six 'Hail Marys' and six 'Glory Be To The Fathers', for each soul to be helped.

Between each individual's rescue, you were required to leave the chapel; each person was a separate visit. The total ritual for each person was to bless yourself, enter the chapel, genuflect, say the novena for a specific person's soul, genuflect and bless yourself with the holy water in the font in the porch, step outside and then restart for the next relative. Each visit ensured a plenary indulgence for the recipient.

I remember Neil specifically because, by the law of coincidence, the summer before I came to live in Derry, Uncle Johnny McHugh from Glenties discovered Uncle Neil alive and well, living in Nazareth House Derry. (On being led by Sister Aidan into a six-bedded room of elderly men, this Donegal voice goes, "Biddie Pheadar Mháire" and that was it). So there are lots of escaped souls up there in the sky demonstrating their gratitude to me by closing up the hole in the ozone layer!

* * *

I was of an age to be a bit obsessed with the concept of 'Indulgences'; I scrutinised the Irish and English prayer books for shortcuts to heaven, (remission of days to be spent in purgatory), naturally selecting ejaculations/prayers for the value of the indulgences/ number of days remission before God (counting and adding the number of days at least improved my mental arithmetic).

However, the important ones were the plenary indulgences guaranteeing getting directly to heaven. Antoine was a great believer in the nine consecutive first Friday Masses St Margaret Mary had promised as a direct route to heaven. His theory was to do them when young and have a licence to party for the rest of your life. However it was Diarmaid who ensured the Morton family received the ultimate plenary indulgence, with a certificate to prove this.

1950 was 'The Holy Year', and a member of each family was, somehow, to visit Rome and receive a Papal Blessing for the family. Diarmaid was about fifteen and himself and Dioraí Ó Corbhinn hitch-hiked to Rome, carrying with them the love and prayers of their families, as well as the official unsigned document which had been authenticated by a local priest and, naturally, written in Irish.

I well remember the day Diarmaid returned home and recognising him only by his horn-rimmed glasses, him proudly giving the parents the official distinctive imprimatur-stamped certificate for Clann Morton. Needless to say this official certificate of our sanctity was framed and hung in pride of place above the sofa in the kitchen – with one exception.

A few years after The Holy Year and the 'big three' at university, Diarmaid and friends started Taibhdhearc Béal Feirste (an Irish Drama group), in the Árd Scoil; with Deirdre, most frequently, as the leading lady.

In the philosophy of 'making use of what you've got', the kitchen sofa and other Morton bits and pieces regularly adorned the stage set, and always, in a prominent position, the framed certificate giving witness to the Belfast Irish-speaking drama fraternity the 'outward sign ' of the 'inward grace' of the Morton family. (Diarmaid and Brigdín, whatever happened the Certificate?)

* * *

I can no longer rely on future generations rescuing my soul from purgatory. I will, therefore, be eternally grateful to Diarmaid for the 1950 Morton family Papal Blessing procuring the direct entry to meet my maker.

Le grá.

XIV

Mongán and Brán

Turmoil – the year Patricia Agnew and I left primary school, her to go to board in Ballycastle with the Cross & Passion nuns and me to Saint Dominic's, signalled the end of my childhood. The rest of the class were staying on until they were 14 and, seemingly, ready to start their working lives.

This move didn't come on its own as that year we moved from my childhood world of Clara Street to the alien environment of South Parade – major upheaval. It wasn't long after this time that Daddy, whose eyesight was always a cause of concern, became blind – the end of the world as I knew it.

There was talk of getting a guide dog and, while those deliberations were happening, a kind, but deluded friend exalted the virtues of a whippet and so Mongán was welcomed in to our home. And yes he was one clever dog, an awesome escapologist (Houdini had nothing on him). Under normal circumstances this might not have been a big problem but Mammy and Mongán locked horns over the sleeping arrangements, he was a house dog, – a very single-minded, totally determined indoor dog and, naturally, Mammy had the expectation of an outdoor-sleeper dog.

We tried all kinds of ruses to get him to sleep in the backyard shed only to be alerted to his escape by the celebratory scratching at the back door; he never made a fuss at being locked in the shed, he probably knew he would escape and it was all a game for him. The escapes I remember best involved an upright tea chest covered with a make-do lid with a heavy box on top and the shed closed. His smile, a minute or two later, at the back door having achieved his goal of the mat in the scullery, while lovingly licking each of us by way of greeting, eventually melted Mammy's heart.

* * *

Did Brán ever go to guide dog school or was he one of their failures? My own idea is that he was simply the runt of a litter of black Labradors who were being bred for training, anyway the main thing was himself and daddy took to each other. With the arrival of Brán, Mongán came in to his own, in that he now had a student to train.

Through a series of nudges, the odd little bite and lots of licks, he taught Brán to sit at Daddy's right side, to nudge his hand to the stand-up ash tray and, most importantly for a peaceful orderly house, to get out from under Mammy's feet.

Mongán taught him that the Rosary was not the time to lick our faces and to lie at peace – but the biggest problem with Brán was that he didn't take to the lead. Clever, multitalented Mongán had the solution to this and I could be found dog walking, myself holding Mongán's lead and Mongán with a tight grip on Brán's lead in his mouth. The Ormeau Embankment was one of the routes and this procession always attracted an appreciative audience; an easy, if bizarre, way of meeting people. Brán's reward was a swim in the Lagan, and Mongán would drag him out for the wet-dog return home.

I think it was for the third or fourth anniversary of Rónán's death that I wanted to be with Cormac and Tracey and they were in New Zealand. While there we went to an outdoor Christmas 'fayre' and I treated myself to an 'authentic' Tarot card reading. The bit I remember was that by the next autumn, my social life would have improved significantly.

Little did I know that by then an undisciplined Scruffy (a black, very-nearly Labrador) would be living with me in long-term foster care. It's true that dog owners are a weird, wonderful, sociable group of people as long as you remember their dog's name, but even my new discipline-water-pistol couldn't hold a candle to Mongán.

XV

The Conway Stewart prize pens

Learning to read was a skill that was caught rather than taught and, thanks to a little water jug advertising Coleraine Whiskey, I caught the reading bug. But learning to write was a skill to be taught; the wooden pen with metal nib, real/powdered ink, blotting paper and the teacher wielding the knuckle ruler, we practiced and practiced.

The schoolroom had long desks with inkwells at each end in the back rows and further up the room the front pupils had individual desks each with its own well. I have to assume that this classroom layout ensured that the teacher didn't get splattered with the ink.

The first task of the day, after prayers and possibly roll call, was the bringing in the correct number of wee milk bottles from the school door. This was, obviously, assigned to the most reliable two or three pupils, not always the teacher's pets but pupils who could count and not drop a bottle. On cold wet days, these were placed near the tepid radiator, other days at the front near the teacher's desk (really the only place there was room, these classrooms were very crowded social environments).

The milk bottle excuse to escape was a much-yearned for job. Then, in eager anticipation, the rest of us waited in our places right hand raised 'my turn Sister/teacher' to receive the jug containing the precious ink to be distributed to each and every inkwell without spilling a drop on the wooden classroom floor.

I often wonder about the monks transcribing The Book of Kells in the candlelight with the white cat Pangur watching, ready to pounce every movement of the quill (or shadow of the quill). Did they never have inkblot disasters like those of us were having with this wee flexible metal nib? Fingers stained with ink, clothes splattered with ink while attempting to balance exactly the amount of liquid needed to scribe a few letters, and so it was that I was frequently sent home with the blue-covered, script-, copy- or half-sized exercise book to practice at home. Being sent to the parlour, a place without distraction – except for the organ – but you were, obviously, caught out when trying to distract yourself trying to play this ancient wheezing machine.

In my memory it was a Wednesday and Daddy must have seen the weary, resigned look on my face as Mammy examined my writing efforts and ordered me to the parlour of oblivion: he produced and, with a flourish, handed me, his black Conway Stewart fountain pen, the fine gold line/band on the lid and the silver lever-valve on the body.

And so began a lifelong, respectful love affair with good pens.

In awe, I opened the pen, put the lid on the body, and opened up this world of clear, clean, blot-less script.

This brought with it two significant learnings; the

ability to fill the pen without upturning the angular bottle of Quink ink and, through my introduction to bartering, how it was that every one of the Mortons could afford and possess these expensive fountain pens. This later was learned by me the year before I started St Dominic's.

My last public act for St Anthony's was to enter the Belfast Féis, all categories – reading, poetry, storytelling, as well as singing. Having spent a year at Magheraroarty on a Gael Linn scholarship, it was assumed, quite rightly, that I would win lots of public/ Irish News acclaim. My own reason for entering all these competitions so willingly was that there were only two 'Morton-permissible', legitimate ways to be out socializing; these were church-led and Irish language activities. And so it was my year, my turn, to be encouraged to 'Féis' at St Mary's Christian Brothers Grammar school on the Falls Road. And yes, I won a pile of Irish books, all of which I recognised from our home book shelves, however, the prizes were minus the official first place labels emblazoned with my name for posterity. I was instructed to take these unadorned prize Féis Irish books to the Ambrose Serridge Bookshop at the bottom of the Falls Road (beside the Continental Cafe) and, on presentation, my understanding was complete. I received my first very own Conway Stewart fountain pen and so I joined the league of blot-less copper-script writers.

The Bic-biro writer will never be able to join this elite tribe.

XVI

Friday nights in South Parade
(Thank you, Emer, for bringing this memory to the surface.)

So many South Parade memories revolve around Daddy's blindness – from my walking the dogs, to himself and Mammy sitting at the aisle seats in the front row of the Holy Rosary Chapel, to making receiving the Eucharist as easy as possible.

The Radio Times in braille was ordered at Brown's Newsagent on the Ormeau Road, and checking the accuracy of the script in whichever Shakespearean play he was reading – the complete works were reread letter by letter in his newly acquired Braille, quite an achievement for him but a bit of a nightmare when required to find a difficult word or phrase in a school edition.

But the lure of winning the football pools, the weekly indulgent gamble, remained and I was given the responsibility of filling in the football coupons. Friday night was 'pools' night, Vernon and/or Liverpool football pool leaflets, collected with the Radio Times on the Thursday, laid out on the table in the kitchen, and two penny-coins were selected for the task. The decision as to whether or not a match was to be a draw (eight draws was the magic figure for the £64,000 windfall) depended on the toss of the coins. Daddy would decide weekly which combination of the toss was to be the draw. So I was to be found, having tossed these pennies which naturally fell onto the floor, on my hands and knees searching for them and calling out 'heads' or 'tails' as appropriate.

I am now so surprised that it never crossed my mind to think of cheating; these coupons had to be filled in in duplicate, one set to be kept and checked on the Saturday when the football results followed the evening news and one to give the pools collector man who collected the coupons and the bet around eight o'clock.

My part in the whole process took a good hour; the coupon held the fixtures for all the English and Scottish divisions, so there was a lot of tossing of coins.

However, once a month the excitement reached new heights, toenail cutting was added to the procedure.

I wouldn't be the greatest foot fan, and in my teens I hadn't yet heard of 'pedicure'. Women's toenails varnished a nice bright red in a high-heeled sandal, those nails I would look at and admire, but daddy's toenails were definitely not of that calibre. Years of wearing 'not quite fitting' shoes had taken their toll.

Before I started the laying out of the football coupons, I brought in a basin of warm water and Epsom Salts for the soaking of the feet. The kettle on the Wellstood range ensured hot water for the top-ups and a towel, cooking in the top oven of the range, for a warm drying.

Keeping the dogs away from the basin and the bare feet involved bribery on my part as both Mongán and Brán wanted to join in the proceedings.

To be honest, Daddy didn't discourage them. It must have been quite an enjoyable experience for him – sitting in a comfortable armchair, feet soaking in warm water, smoking an Embassy Red or two, with the dogs' heads in his lap while this youngest child carried out the football pools ritual. The post-pools toenail-cutting wasn't that difficult or traumatic, despite the tickle in his fee, and the warmed towel on the floor captured the slivers. Feet were dried and a big sigh of relief that I hadn't done any permanent damage – and that was why I decided to be a psychologist and not a chiropodist.

Le grá.

XVII

The Tyrone connection

One dominant image of relatives visiting Clara Street, and later South Parade, is the feathered rooster hanging by its spurs on a hook in the scullery, the bright red comb glistening and swaying: the prospect of pulling the feathers and cleaning out the innards to use the heart and gizzards to make real gravy (my favourite part of the chicken dinner). Only after taking in this full scenario did I wonder if it was Mary Jack, whom I was slightly afraid of, or Auntie Annie (Mammy's sister, Killen, Coalisland, County Tyrone) – in which case there would be eggs for tea.

I think Mary Jack, whom I always associate with dirty wellington boots, was one of the Donegal third cousins X-times removed – like the O'Gradys. However, Auntie Annie and family were as influentially dominant in my life as the image of the red rooster comb. Somehow, I always sensed that Annie totally disapproved that we were being reared with, and spoke, Irish. Although she must have been a native speaker, I never heard her speak Irish, it was as if it was a part of her 'to be dismissed/repressed', past history. Uncle Paddy however was an astute businessman, a Nationalist councillor, with a dry Tyrone sense of humour. (I read, with great glee, in the Irish News the excuse given when late for a council meeting: he was following a rabbit running up the middle of the road and didn't want to knock it down!)

Even before they began breeding greyhounds in one of their many garages, the McGraths had a host of money-making industries. Financial security and social status were important to Auntie Annie – from contributing the most money to Church collections to two sons becoming priests. And, as for Mammy, not a potential priest or nun between us.

So this complicated relationship was Mammy trying to seek Annie's approval and the McGraths needing the extra education that Daddy could provide, with us, three wee ones, as bargaining chips to help with cleaning their house, general light farm work but not up to the required standard to work in their shop/post-office.

And so school holiday times, when not heading to the Gaeltacht, my usefulness as a cleaner and general dogsbody would see me getting the bus to Dungannon where I would sit in Uncle Paddy's building contractor's office, with a sophisticated cup of tea, until it was time for him to go home to the Killen crossroads for a Mary Foster fry. Gathering at the crossroad in the evening was still the tradition and more than compensated for any daytime toil. Bicycles were the primary source of transport and Mary Foster, who had a motor on hers, ensured flattering male attention for herself and her entourage.

* * *

And so it was with Hugh well on the way to parish priesthood, Sean in Dalgan preparing for the foreign missions, that it was Patrick's turn to have possession of the small bedroom at the top of the stairs (the single "boys room").

Sometime, during one of these working holidays, I kind of wondered about the reality of Patrick's hair, but it was a shock to realise the truth. One day, just the once, there sitting on the bed spread was a glorious ginger wig. I'm not sure what happened when he was playing Gaelic, and all the McGrath boys starred in the Clonoe parish teams in all sports, but I saw the ginger wig with my own eyes and I couldn't unsee it.

I think Colm had started breeding greyhounds while he was still at St Patrick's Armagh and, by the time I heard about his success, inscribed Waterford glass trophies in pristine condition adorned every nook and cranny of his and Mary's home opposite Clonoe chapel.

And so, everyone in the parish benefited financially from the winner of the Irish Greyhound Derby, and her nearly equally famous sister, and when their racing days were coming to an end breeding was the next lucrative plan. It so happened we, us Downeys, were visiting at the time both greyhounds had produced litters.

Our Derry experience of dog litters was of the 'do you know anyone who wants a pup?'-variety, so it was natural for Garbhán to say, "We'll take one." In the broad rural Tyrone accent of the ten-year-old son/

grandson came the put-down response to silence all non-millionaires, "They're coming from Saudi Arabia to see these pups."

My own put-down – Tyrone people are experts at deflating your bubble – came about when I was driving the wee red Fiat 126 and was conducting the research into Adult Literacy provision. This found me paying a quick visit to Auntie Annie at Killen Crossroads. I pulled in front of the house between the two silver Mercedes and the two silver Rover cars.

I think it was Paul (but Paul, Colm and Patrick were all out seeing me off) leaned the two elbows on the roof of a Merc, looked at my tiny car, and said, "Isn't education the wonderful thing?" I got into the hairdryer and was simply relieved it started, and off I went.

Auntie Annie, God love her, never lost her need for status. The last time I spent time with her was at Uncle Paddy's wake. She wasn't well enough to go to the chapel at the removal of Paddy's remains. I volunteered to stay so that all the family members could all be present.

I sat up in the bed beside her and as soon as the front door closed, I was instructed to open a blind and I held her hand as she counted the cars as the procession wound its way to Clonoe Chapel.

Le grá.

XVIII

Parcels from America

Virtually all Irish families have relatives in America; much has been recorded about emigration at the time of 'the Great Hunger', and since, through the effects of poverty and unemployment. In the Morton family, while we knew we had relatives there, I have no growing-up memory of any contact.

My doll with the china face came in a parcel from America to the Agnew's. The excitement in a home when 'a parcel' arrived was a sight to behold. These parcels of clothes, precious nylons, toys and goodies kept hope alive in many, many Irish homes and contained the essentials, and the fought-over luxuries, of most Christmas stockings.

* * *

Early 1970s. 'Twas the day before the night before Christmas; Santa and the elves were searching out the presents for Earlswood Road, and the mice were worrying about how safe it would be to fly the sled, avoid the fighting in Belfast, and ensure safe delivery of gifts for the four daughters who'd posted their letters up the chimney in good time; Brigdín and Pat made sure of that.

This human parcel from America was pacing

the streets off the Newtownards Road looking for Mrs Morton (nee McDermott), her of the long McBrearty back. We had always talked about the 'long McDermott back' but the ancestral genes were on Neanaí's mother's side of the family.

There was a before-that beginning in which the Mortons played no active part, however, we were passively used by a McGrath relative to promote their family status, and credibility of oppression, further up in the American social importance. Killen, Coalisland wasn't getting the USA headlines during the 'Troubles' whereas having relatives in Belfast and Derry were important 'feathers in the caps' of some Irish-Americans. Yes, one consequence of having the media attention.

I have always assumed the offending relative who gave us away to be Father Sean McGrath, who visited America on his way home from the missions after a second or third seven-year stretch in the Philippines. It seems the priest had access to sources of information for long-lost relations and, to be honest, he was very proud of his Donegal/Irish roots.

This pride he demonstrated when he first went to the Philippines – he hadn't realised that hurling wasn't one of their native sports and so thirty-plus camáns and sliotars were immediately requested and sent; and, with him now being responsible for the education of Catholic children, the Morton family in Clara Street were responsible for the sending of multiple copies of 'Na Rossa go bráth' by Máire, the naivety of us all, but a change from collecting pennies for 'the black babies'.

So Fr Sean, without consulting us innocent Mortons, assured the long-lost American relatives of a warm safe welcome, provided the address of Neanaí, possibly the existence of Conways and Downeys but, somehow, failed to give the addresses of his immediate Tyrone relatives. In his defence, having been away, he wasn't to know/realise the kudos of access to direct and personal research in the NI Troubles for American college students.

* * *

And so the day before the day before Christmas, I heard from a "Do you know anything about this?" Brigdín – that a human parcel, Peter Mac, was there with two arms the one length and, as soon as travel services were back to normal, they would see him on his way to Derry: at least we had some warning. Given that I was in the throes of collating the results section of my research over the Christmas break, when Garbhán and Rónán were in bed, and Derry was in the throes of bombings – his comments on the superiority of American research weren't really appreciated by me. His expectation was that we would be delighted to be treating him to food and drink and honoured by his presence. However, almost adding insult to our insignificance to his life, he did show the colour of his money by buying John Hume a drink. There's an expression 'if you can't say something nice say nothing', and so my lips are tied.

After the New Year, I phoned the McGraths and escorted him to the Dungannon bus. I have been told that they brought him to the races and left him there.

Anyway, who needs parcels from America when you can have Irish-speaking hurlers in the Philippines?

Le grá.

XIX

Coming of Age
Tirupati, India

I was awakened by the rhythmical jingling of the elephants' foot bells as they are led into the town for the dawn ceremony at the main temple. I must be becoming familiar with this environment, as the mosquito net around the bed no longer seems claustrophobic. The roof fan isn't humming – the electricity is off again. I wonder if Ireland really is 4,000 miles away. Anyway, X-thousand miles away, the eldest son is 18 today. I decide not to cry but to get up and watch the sunrise spectacular from the roof garden of the university guesthouse. It's a truly amazing, even vulgar, display of the magnificence of God, playing with the creativity of humanity, in sculpting temples to catch each changing hue.

The entrance to the garden is blocked by a very large grey female monkey. She seems to be sleeping and as I try to circumvent her, she utters a "one false move and you'll have me to answer to" growl. I can see she's hurt and I now know why there is no electricity. Her two chimps cling to my legs and are demanding that I do something.

"Look I'm no vet, but I don't think there is much even a vet could do. I'll stay with you, it'll be alright."

I sit down on the dewy grass inside the garden. I stay very still making soothing noises, while they lift her ear and scratch her back uttering plaintive keening noises. Eventually they return to me and take my hands. We walk over to the corpse and I tell them how sorry I am, and how useless I feel and that I don't know what to say.

After a while their keening calms down, and we go for a gentle quiet walk around the garden.

I hear a door opening. The dreadful history professor's room is more or less directly opposite the roof garden. Out of the corner of my eye, I see the man in vest and underpants lift his doormat and fling it at the mother. The mat is followed by a couple of books. By now the chimps are clinging round my neck, screeching in rage and terror.

"There's no need to be afraid, I'll make sure he won't get near you, he's just a stupid ignorant person," I find myself saying, with a calmness that I do not feel.

The immediate danger of my face getting clawed apart passes, to be rapidly followed by more tight clinging and jabbering, reacting to a commotion on the stairs. The houseboys, still in their nightshirts, armed with brushes and an assortment of kitchen equipment, are sidling up the stairs with the professor courageously taking up the rear position.

"High Noon time," says I to myself as I make my presence visible.

"Please don't any of you move, you can see the monkey is dead; these chimps are a bit emotional."

I didn't have to say anymore as the chimps were baring their teeth and spitting fury in the general direction of the pathetic-looking line.

I unwrap the chimps from the half-nelson clutches on my neck, they take my hands and we walk back into the garden. Enormous Professor Raza has been wakened by the commotion. I might have known he would have an exotic nightshirt. He lumbers into the garden, sits down where it joins the jungle and indicates that I bring the chimps over. Someone makes a move on the stairs; the chimps will have none of it. Calm again; we walk, with chimps taking it in turns to look backwards, and make our way to the corner. "We need to sit quietly here."

He's not moving his upper lip when he speaks and I pretend not to notice the obvious missing tooth. "The relatives are out there in the bushes, they'll call for the chimps to join them when they know it's safe."

We sit and discuss the meaning of life and whether or not God makes mistakes. The chimps seem to find the discourse interesting, except when anyone on the stairs fidgets. There's a rustling in the bushes and then some noises that the chimps are reacting to. We continue talking, an Indian man and an Irish woman, on the similarities and differences of our lives – the conversation in the bushes is the one the chimps are listening to.

They let go of my hands and jump. We formally shake hands, Professor Raza and me, the line of men on the stairs drift away. I go to my room and send the telepathic message to the eldest son, "Go for it. Jump." And then I cry.

Le grá.

XX

Richie Morton in Tirupati

The train journey travelling inland from Madras to Tirupati, a distance of about 300 miles, first-class travel, my memory is that I stood at the glassless window holding on to the bars wondering what in under of God I was doing: I gradually came to the realisation that I was going to the Graffy that my mother grew up in.

I had been in India maybe thirty hours and knew I needed to get my head sorted, a perspective I could relate to, and I must admit that when I found the Morton-McDermott family connection, the situation seemed to make a bit of sense. It was the fact that the first appointment made for me was to go to the temple to meet the Hindu priests in order to be given permission to meet the local women that sparked the 'Mammy growing up and the power of the priests in rural Ireland' train-of-thought and gave me a perspective; so the staring out the train window was not in vain.

Such a welcome I got as I was getting off the train, I was totally enveloped in a warm smelly hug, Daddy's distinctive smell – mentholatum, Mrs Collins headache powders, Gallagher's Blues and Lifebuoy Soap, Daddy greeting me on the platform of Tirupati train station, and then I heard Professor Philomena Reddy call my name.

I had expected the battle with the mosquitos to last until I tuned in to their buzz and perfected the finger flick, and the bed bugs were easily disposed of with a nightly energetic balcony mattress beating followed by a dose of Milton, but the white ant was a different story. Its favourite food was the lump of gum freshly placed outside the post office to glue the stamp and the aerogram sheet for the letters. The middle finger of the right hand squashed hundreds of ants to accompany each and every letter home.

Letters from home were a source of great joy to myself as well as the students, and photographs were deeply appreciated by the worshippers in the long queues to the temples of the Hindu Gods especially Lord Venketswara – where the women left the gift of their long black tresses.

The first letter from Garbhán, Rónán and Cormac started with 'the days are very long without you' followed by long amusing descriptions of the problems with milk and bread. The aerograms, a single sheet, couldn't really contain a full story of life in Tirupati, even with tiny writing, so under the guidance of my father, I would start a letter to one Morton family member and tell them whom to contact for the rest of the news/story! Daily the students would ask me how Daddy was doing; they didn't find it in any way strange that he was here with me telling me whom to write to next. As for my letters home, you didn't ask anyone to post them; the squashed ant scenario was a personal, very personal, act of love; it certainly gave positive motivation to rise early to try to catch the postman as the white-ant-delicacy of gum was placed outside.

In the early letters home, I would request that the steaks in the freezer be replaced and I had just reached the stage of 'oh for a bowl of cornflakes and cold milk', when I received a letter from Deirdre full of the forthcoming Laoise Confirmation and anticipating whether the pledge would last the celebratory evening meal. (This letter I was able to give to Laoise when she was expecting Sona Deirdre).

I explained to these Hindu students the ritual of the Confirmation pledge, I described the relationship of Gráinne, Dunla and Laoise with Deirdre in loving detail, as a result of which one female student who was so sorry that I did not have daughters told me she would be my daughter while I was in India.

The thought of a celebratory meal awoke in me the anticipation of Deirdre's cooking that set my taste-buds on fire; my diet at the time consisted of lots of bananas/plantain with each meal, loads of vegetables and spices, no meat (especially since I saw a scraggy goat being led into the butchers) and, to wash it down, cold boiled water.

I tried to describe to these vegetarian students the lengthy, complicated preparation of Deirdre's home-made pâté served on freshly toasted wheaten bread (all of her cooking was lengthy and complex), but it is the baffled incredulous look on their faces when I was describing Deirdre making her Baked Alaska that sticks in the memory.

The final letters I wrote were to Antoine, and then Diarmaid and Brigdín. Daddy was nagging me to tell Antoine that he was to continue to work at keeping in contact with his sons, and because he was still poking at me, I wrote wee letters to Brigdín and Diarmaid to let them know that I had told Daddy to tell them whatever the message was – that he was trying to tell me something but I couldn't hear; those letters arrived around the time of Deirdre's funeral.

It was Rónán who got through on the phone to tell me Deirdre was dead and it was the Indian daughter and her friends who packed the bag and made sure there were gifts for everyone, while Philomena Reddy and some of the older students stayed with me and arranged a short prayerful ritual in which each child and sibling got prayed for by name, and especially Richie, whose constant presence ensured everyone had been in contact during the post-Christmas-fallow-time.

Le grá.

XXI

A Morton miracle at Lourdes?

It was the summer after Deirdre died, after Cormac made his First Communion, around the time Fionnuala walked the Camino (the first person I knew to walk this pilgrimage), and Gemma wanted to bring her mother Kathleen to Lourdes. I have never had any ambition to go there, nor had I any intention of going there, but at the last moment her 'helper' couldn't go, and I certainly did not want to disappoint Kathleen.

So, three miles outside of Derry, there I was seated on a pilgrimage bus on route to Dublin airport when a priestly microphoned voice started the Rosary, not a bead in my pocket and everyone else in a state of pious readiness. This devotion lasted until we reached the Duty Free and, I must admit, I was mildly astonished at the quantity of spirits being bought, presumably for a wee nightcap or two after a day of praying. Duty Free conversations consisted of 'last year we ran out of…are you sure that's enough….ach, poor so-and-so, she loved her wee glass of Baileys.' The chatter was akin to the whooper swans arriving back in Burt for the winter and conducting a noisy bird-head count of survivors.

* * *

The day's ceremonies centred around the officially sick, and we all stood aside in reverence to ensure they had, with their helpers, preferential seating in the cathedral, then the rest of us filed in. The contradiction to such respect for the sick and infirm came at completion of a service when you could see us trip over anyone and everyone to escape for a few minutes before it was time to gather for the next organised ritual of the pilgrimage.

It was after a few days, and people buying rosary beads and queuing to light blessed candles that the realisation hit me that Lourdes was full of revelations and contradictions about our human condition and that the only card I would send would be to India; everyone else could visit if they wanted.

Each pilgrimage is allocated a special time for the miracle water baths; you don't bring a towel as you rise from the bath dry. The exit to the baths was lined with discarded crutches as the outward signs of past miracles. In our pilgrimage we passed a few humorous remarks to each other on the dry-water experience but that was our only obvious miracle sign – I am sure our inward grace grew in strength.

The revelation of faith I found on going to the Grotto late in the evening and being with the real pilgrims who intended to remain in prayer there for the night; such was the strength of devotion, of their total trust, belief and devotion, this was awe inspiring – the memory still sends shivers down the spine. In this desolate, lonely place a person could believe

that a mother would go to such a wild incongruous/
inconspicuous place and shout at the world for not
listening to her son – at a human level many a mother
has gone to a wild place and shouted to the wind or
to anyone who would listen about the frustration of
no one listening/heeding her son's potential – yes the
Derry mother could see this would be a good shouting
place: and yet the faith of these night pilgrims touched
something deep inside the soul.

Irish pilgrimages are booked to say a special mass
at St Patrick's church as part of their devotions, and
that was how I found myself being quite disheartened,
about to be singing of the glory of Ireland, having just
left Derry in the throes of 'the Troubles'. So I quietly left
the chapel and was looking at the gravestones when a
very familiar aroma hit me – it was one of our group, a
priest's homemaker/housekeeper and her 'thin enough
for one eye'. But it was Deirdre's very distinctive
aroma that caused me to ask her how she was. The
symptoms she described seemed very familiar to the
long-standing eating discomfort that Deirdre suffered
for many years and, as with Deirdre, there was no
known cause. I told her of the undiagnosed growth on
Deirdre's adrenal gland, and how it was the distinctive
smell I was reacting to. Strange that we didn't exchange
names, well Derry people don't, we simply comforted
each other until the others came out of the mass. As far
as I was concerned, I rejoined Gemma and Kathleen
with some excuse for leaving the Mass.

* * *

It was a few months later the 'bean gan ainm' made sure I got the word, on the grapevine, that her operation was successful.

XXII

The years of the nuns

Before starting to write this I was only thinking about the Dominicans – the Cross & Passion nuns didn't figure in my thinking; and then the memories resurrected themselves. During one of my sojourns in Senior Infants and Sister Mary Francis paying me unnecessary and unreciprocated affection/attention I concluded that uncle Neil had jilted her, left her at the altar and, as a result of her broken heart, she had entered the nunnery! And here she was with us (especially me) as her substitute children whom she could smother with her affection.

Totally logical thinking for this four or five maybe six-year old and I think I continued to believe this well into adulthood but had the wit not to give voice to it. However, at odd times in my adult life this belief did reoccur.

Additionally the big deep pockets in the full length black habits of the Cross & Passion nuns of Saint Anthony's, Willowfield worried me. These pockets could swallow up a small child and at three years of age I was a very small child.

My first school memory: there I am stood at the front of the class beside Sister Mary Francis adjacent to the big pockets with her right arm across my shoulders in an ill-practiced hug – I was petrified.

My big learning with the Cross & Passion Nuns was how to avoid being punished. Brigdín was slapped with a wooden pointer by a nun whose anger was her only contribution to our education, and this anger with her world was ever present: having seen this terrible slapping I was quietly, oh so very quietly, determined that this would never ever happen to me.

At this early age I realised that any schooling failure would be 'letting down the family name' so I made sure I learned to do whatever was required to achieve, to stay out of trouble, and to be good at running messages for the teacher. I'm still good at running the messages!

I hadn't that long started St Dominic's when Daddy, coming out of teaching in Oxford Street Primary School suddenly couldn't see – detached retina – and so, visits to Moorfields Eye Hospital, London for both parents. It was after the second or third series of operations that the realisation came that nothing more could be done and Daddy was now blind. Sister Philomena, the domestic science teacher (who really objected to the fact that I had chosen to study science rather than domestic) baked us the Christmas cake, the first cake professionally-iced I remember. And the teaching order of Dominicans thought of themselves as the epitome of professionalism.

At school with the Dominican nuns, I was absorbing that they were promoting two classes of women; superior nuns (the moneyed, educated teachers) had bells to summon them to prayer, class or whatever, the lesser the number of rings the higher up the celestial strata you were; whereas the lay sisters (those who entered without a dowry) were simply verbally ordered around by their superiors'. Even in my teens while recognising that life in the world was more difficult for women anyway, I resented the idea that these nuns were making life even more difficult for 'poor' women', who entered the nunnery simply to serve God or escape their world. (I must acknowledge that it was thanks to the dowries that there was post-primary education for girls in Belfast.)

* * *

These Dominicans, except for Sr Philippa, didn't value our being Irish; European preferably, British as second best, but our Irishness was unacknowledged. There was a dearth of Irish authors in the school library, and we learned to dance the Gay Gordons, and not the sixteen-hand reel during the wet lunch hours.

Why or how I got onto the hockey team is a bit of a mystery, Brigdín was a much better player than I was, but it served the purpose of my learning the how-to-protest-effectively process.

The pinnacle of Dominican pupil respectability was to be a 'child of Mary'; over the white shirt the blue ribbon was your personal outward sigh of superiority – spiritual, academic, everyway. It wasn't automatic in senior year and I have no idea about the selection procedure; in my case I was definitely nominated for the accolade, however betwixt cup and lip I was informed that the confraternity-type meetings would always be a Saturday morning – well that was hockey match time.

Wednesday after school and Saturday mornings were my legitimate escape from housework; getting to see parts of the 'world' I would never otherwise have access to, after the match – up the town – the adolescent pride of a sophisticated cup of coffee in Whites…. all this was in my life thanks to the 'playing hockey' experience. As against this, never to wear the precious blue ribbon or the possibility of being a prefect, a 'house' captain and definitely doomed never to be head or deputy-head girl.

Of course, the outside world won and with it never having to pretend again that I would become a nun. But telling the horrified nuns that I was selling my soul to worldly considerations? It was at this stage that the realisation came to me that we were the only Catholic school playing hockey, in my mind not simply playing with Protestants in their schools but actually beating them; not only was this a one-up for us Catholics it was also a step closer to a united Ireland.

Strange how selling my soul to the devil was never referred to when the team was being congratulated for drawing in the cup final with Belfast Royal Academy, with photographs in the papers.

At the time standing there, and saying No to the precious blue ribbon with the medal attached – in my eyes this was a 'Joan of Arc' moment.

* * *

However, it was as one first girls doing science subjects that showed the school at its creative best. Thinking outside the box to make the maximum use of what you had wasn't yet a popular educational way of thinking, and in 1959 I'm not sure any other group of teaching professionals would have even tried.

There were three of us in the Advanced Level Physics class and two in the Chemistry class and both subjects had practical tests (equipment lent for the occasion by St Mary's Boys School the day before the examination) with external examiners. Not having equipment in physics (apologies St Dominic's, we did have prisms) simply meant a lot of 'learning off' diagrams/angles/formulae, but titration for chemistry was another matter. The solution for Ann McGarrity and myself (both singers) was music – hold the pipette nozzle open for a quaver/semi-quaver/crochet, and while the examiner might have wanted to hush our sporadic outbursts of musical notes – we both passed with flying colours.

So there I was, ready to take on the world – armed with a fierce need to please, knowing how to write a letter to the Pope, how to eat an orange at a Spanish banquet and that nuns have ankles but my real armoury was how to say no, how to stand up for myself, how women can put other women down and the most enduring weapon was to make fulsome use of what I had.

Two Poems

Crystal Light and Snowdrops
For Rónán

Leaning on
My Dear Palestrina
The photograph of you
Playing the baby grand
In the piano room circa 1980s

While waiting for the
TG4 people to…
This isn't about you, a Rúin
It's about the Hospice
And the way you used it
To help family and friends
Come to understand
That you knew
Your illness was terminal

To the Hospice you brought light
Crystal light
Spectrums dancing on the beds
Bringing rainbows
To the mortally ill.

In hindsight you brought
The light of understanding
Making the meaning of Hospice

'Biseacht an bháis'
So crystal clear.

And a memory is of
Bishop Daly carrying a pot of
Mary Clinton's snowdrops
To your teacher Theresa Bryce –
Snowdrops now growing
On the banks of Loughgall

Grá
Áine x

Putting time aside
For Cormac

Between 13. 04. 01 and
14. 04. 01,
Carrying with me
The love of Garbhán, Úna, Fiachra, Gerry
And the presence of Rónán
I crossed the equator
And God Neptune did not appear
To come to celebrate
This crossing.

Fables of childhood,
The mystical ceremony of the crossing,
The godly acknowledgement, recognition
Of moving across the earth-line
Into the other unknown world.
Imagined ceremony, ritual
Other world connectedness.
Childhood illusion shattered
On a flight from Bangkok to Sydney
In the 'putting time aside' time
Towards the reality of coming
Nearer and nearer to wonderful Cormac.

This first Easter of Rónán
Connected with the other world,
This human-godly other world connectedness
And the knowing that the touching

In these human relationships
Is the God Neptune ceremony
Of moving across the earth-line.

Grá
Áine x

In Continuum

The Morton who spoke Macedonian

Áine was in the throes of compiling the new edition of her book, when she died in the kitchen of her home on a beautiful May evening, aged 77. She had been savouring the relaxation of the Covid lockdown restrictions, which meant she could walk to the park with her beloved Scruffy and visit the rest of us for Sunday lunch again. In the days before she passed away, she had been cooking dinners for Gerry, who was ill, and had enjoyed a two-hour long, sun-kissed tea party in the garden with her granddaughter Brónagh.

Áine had spoken often about her mortality and was completely unafraid. In all respects, her death was exactly as she had pre-ordered – without suffering, 'fuss' or debility. Despite issues with her heart and encroaching ischemia – she lost part of her left foot in 2019 – she was still rigorously independent and mentally sharp as a tack. For all that – and for all we feel her legacy and spirit in our lives, we miss her terribly.

Áine never saw great age as her entitlement, pointedly describing life after threescore years and ten as 'bonus time'. The Mortons are renowned for their vascular frailty – three of Áine's siblings died in their fifties, (Deirdre at just 52, Antoine at 59 and Máire Róisín at 59), while her father Richie was only 66.

Áine was much loved and hugely respected in her adopted Derry home, with friends from the 'Seven Streets' neighbourhood dyeing their hair or beards pink in her honour, before applauding her cortege into and out of St Eugene's Cathedral. (She had been colouring her grey hair pink for the past decade or more – and was known in Lidl as The Punk Granny.)

There were also scores of tributes to her from all sorts of people working in all sorts of sectors all over the world. She had no regrets and had left nothing undone or unsaid. The Irish News headline of the funeral reported: 'Academic was "strong, fearless and free".'

* * *

When we produced the first print of the book in 2019, it was as a Christmas surprise for Áine. We suspected (rightly) that she would much prefer us to keep the focus on her writing – and not on her extraordinary life, so our introduction was functional and not-at-all effusive. Áine was modest about her achievements and wouldn't have thanked us for a hagiography. So it wasn't until we were preparing some notes for her funeral celebrant Fr Paul Farren that we truly started to consider just how much of a trailblazer Áine had been.

As you will read in this memoir, she went to primary school in Belfast, at St Anthony's, Willowfield and then on to St Dominic's College on the Falls Road, (where she played Camogie for Antrim minors). But her mother, Brigid, was a great believer in the merits of the Southern education system, and so, aged just eight, Áine upped sticks on her own to attend a Donegal national school for a year, on an Irish language scholarship.

Her early academic career was ground-breaking but always with an extremely practical focus. After taking a science degree at Queen's (BSc, II.i, 1964) and publishing a paper on physiological psychology, she began investigating the difficulties faced by children 'whose intellectual disabilities are more obvious than my own'. She then used this research to challenge the powers-that-be – the churches, the education authorities or the health services – to meet their responsibilities rather than closing doors.

As a governor of Belmont Special School (she was on the board there for 50 years) she lobbied, successfully, for pupils to be allowed to receive church sacraments such as Holy Communion and Confirmation. She also fought the education department to ensure 'statemented' pupils had the right to sit mainstream exams; one of her proudest moments was when a young woman with Down's syndrome she had previously mentored was awarded a degree.

Áine's doctorate (NUU, 1973), entitled 'Educational Subnormality: Etiology and Stimulation Level', was centred on resolving the specific learning problems facing 'ESN' children between the ages of eleven to fourteen. Some of the standardised terms used in the 250-page thesis would make you wince today – Áine, herself, led the campaign to get rid of many of these definitions. She was a lifelong believer in never putting labels on children. Some well-meaning members of the establishment later attempted to persuade Áine to accept a 'gong' for her services to special education, but she discreetly – and firmly – turned them down.

* * *

Áine first moved to Derry in 1964, the year she got married, securing a teaching job at St Mary's Secondary School in Creggan, where she had responsibility for a number of 'ESN' classes. She began teaching part-time at Magee in 1967, becoming a full-time researcher in 1969 and a lecturer in 1970. She used to joke that she worked for four universities from the same office – Trinity College, Magee University College, the New University of Ulster (NUU) and the University of Ulster (UU).

Besides lecturing and serving on the university's Council, she supervised numerous doctoral theses and devised hosts of new courses, including the first ever accredited diploma on Addiction Studies at UU. She also taught on Magee's revolutionary Foundation Studies diploma, which was responsible for giving hundreds of mature students an entry-route into third-level education. In the late 1980s and early 1990s, Magee enjoyed a spurt of growth, during which time Áine helped oversee the reintroduction of undergraduate degrees to the campus. (All undergraduate courses had been moved out of Derry to Coleraine in the late 1960s.)

In the 1980s, she spent a number of months as a visiting professor at the Sri Venkateswara University in Tirupati, South East India, returning from her sabbatical after the unexpected death of her eldest sister Deirdre. She loved to travel and would later work on a British Council project in Nigeria. She also visited friends and relatives all over the world from the remote edges of the Arctic to the Equator; though her favourite journey was always to northwest England to see Cormac and Tracey, and her Mancunian grandsons Bertie and Elwood.

* * *

A number of Áine's students at Magee were paramilitaries, or former paramilitaries, from both sides of the North's community. She would recall fascinating and important, highly-charged debates taking place – in the sanctuary of a lecture room – between republicans and loyalists, and was devastated at the killing of former student, a UDA commander shot dead in 1976.

While moving house in Derry in the mid-1980s, she became a live-in staff warden at student halls in Derry. During this time she helped co-ordinate Magee's emergency response after an IRA attack on the campus left a part-time student (a prison officer) and two policemen dead. She opened up her big living room as a communal dorm for students to bring in their sleeping bags – and brewed up massive pots of her legendary chicken soup to help settle them.

When she subsequently condemned the attack on television, the republican movement did not challenge her. She had supervised many of them, visited and taught others in jail, and even testified in court on behalf of a number. She resolutely believed in non-violence, and that schools and universities must always remain protected spaces, and did not shirk from saying this.

Áine was actually teaching a student in Crumlin Road prison the day of the big escape from the jail in 1981. She was coming back home over the Glenshane Mountain in her little Fiat 126 when she heard the news on the radio. And she had to put up with many jokes about how she had smuggled the eight escapees back to Derry in the boot.

* * *

Because of her position as a teacher and her talent as a principled persuader, Áine always believed she had a responsibility to do what she could to better her community. In the early 1980s, she accepted a nomination to the board of the Inner City Trust, to help restore and regenerate the urban landscape that had been decimated by war.

Her concern at the damage being done by alcohol and drugs on families across the North West led her to serve as a director of Northlands, Derry's addiction treatment centre.

Then in 1984, the Northern Ireland Secretary Jim Prior asked her to join the new Standing Advisory Commission on Human Rights for Northern Ireland.

And despite reservations about its possible efficacy, she agreed on the basis that she believed Prior had integrity and that the commission needed at least one representative who was 'Catholic, female, west of the Bann'.

* * *

Some of her most creative ideas were inspired by her personal experience. Her father Richie had lost his sight in his early fifties, and this motivated her to get involved at the ground floor with Derry's Talking Newspaper for the Blind, which has now been running in the city for more than forty years.

She lived more than half of her life within 200 yards of Brooke Park and, alongside a host of other activists, was at the heart of the community drive to regenerate it in recent years. The park's eventual multi-million pound restoration was a source of great pride to her – particularly as she then got to enjoy it every day on her walks with Scruffy. And she loved nothing better than the panoramic view of the city from the new park café where she could meet friends and family for brunch. If the warden wasn't about, she was more than happy to deal with the occasional teenage drinking party by wandering over, harmless little old lady, and handing them a packet of bin bags to clean up after themselves. And she would remind them to be sure and only use the indoor toilets so as not to be scaring the families using the park.

Likewise, Rónán's illness prompted her to volunteer at the Foyle Hospice, where she worked as a sous-chef in the kitchen one morning a week for years. She was a marvellous cook; her mother had been a great baker and Áine inherited a host of family recipes. At Crawford Square, when we were growing up, she was the most hospitable of hosts at her open house-slash-safe haven*. There was always a big pot of soup on the stove, and homemade shepherd's pies or meat pies in the freezer, for starving teens, late-night revellers and passing friends. (*Áine would quietly hand spare keys of her house to women and men who might be going through a rough time, and always have the spare room made up, so they would have a safe place to stay.) But it is as a jam-maker that she will have lasting culinary fame – supplying half of Ráth Mór every autumn with her homemade preserves; plum, apple, blackberry and rhubarb – all from home-grown fruit.

* * *

In 1995, after thirty years as an academic, Áine declared that she had had enough of school and took early retirement from UU, delighting in the fact that they would now pay her not to come in every day. She then began a second career in public service, and spent the next twenty-five years as an independent champion in the education and health sectors.

Her first big project as a 'free agent' was to help set up Lifestart, a developmental programme to assist parents educating their young children in the home. Initially, Lifestart branches were established in areas of greatest social and economic need. So Áine travelled to a red-light district in Barcelona to set up a pilot for young mothers there, and later headed to the post-war Balkans to launch a branch in Skopje. It was Cormac who remembered how Áine had actually learnt Macedonian from tapes in the car for her trip. (And they must have understood her well, because that Skopje branch is still running today.)

Áine served two four-year terms on the Western Education and Library Board, leading its pioneering pre-school expansion programme, and two terms on the Western Health Board, including one as Deputy-Chair. She also sat on the Mental Health Review Tribunal for Northern Ireland, was a director of the Armagh Planetarium, and served as a governor for numerous schools.

She was renowned on committees for her ability to cut through regulatory gobbledygook and ask solution-focused questions. Importantly, her strong background in mathematics meant she was also great with accounts, from the most complex to petty cash. When 'the girls' were going out for their monthly dinner, they would always hand the bill to Áine to divvy it up at the end. Once when an interviewer condescendingly asked Áine what experience she had managing large budgets, she told him had been a single mother running a household for twenty years and had never once been overdrawn.

In 2000, Áine was appointed by the Department

of Education to sit on the Burns Review into Post Primary Education, which recommended scrapping selection by academic ability – i.e. the end of the 11-Plus. The Department was impressed with her eye for detail – her first rule was to proofread any document she was presented and send it back if it had any spelling mistakes – so much so that she was then re-engaged as a consultant by the DE when it was establishing the North's new state-wide Education Authority.

Her love of Irish was never far away, however, and in 2000 she became a founding director of Comhairle na Gaelscolaíochta, the representative body for Irish-medium education in the North, and also joined the board of Cultúrlann uí Chanáin in Derry. Her spelling in Irish, she conceded, should always be checked – ditto the grammar. For her, it was a spoken language – and she never got a proper handle on the new 'Caighdeán Oifigiúil' (official standard), which was introduced in the 1950s.

* * *

Áine took her Catholicism seriously, though questioned its hierarchy, insisting that 'the Church' was the people and not the structures. She would occasionally challenge her Mass companions, by announcing 'Our Creator' when the priest would be beginning the 'Our Father'. But despite her occasional fights with God, and a misguided attempt by one cleric to refuse her Communion after her divorce, she remained a fixture in the Irish language choir, Cór an Ghrianán, until her death. She adored music (her middle son, our late brother Rónán, once starred as a musical prodigy in a BBC film with Liam Neeson), and she had planned to have the Belmont school choir sing at her funeral, but the lockdown made that impossible.

* * *

A voracious reader – Áine enjoyed everything from the Booker list to cheesy magazines (they helped her switch off) – it irked her that her eyes began to fail in later years. This meant she had to stop driving, which she did voluntarily, even if she immediately began looking for an electric scooter.

There would be no stopping her writing letters, cards, emails, texts, Facebook posts and Tweets, however. Her children, siblings, nieces and nephews, godchildren, grandchildren and many friends will testify that she never missed a birthday, feast day or the chance to help someone or brighten their day. A gadget lover, she embraced new technology and social media and, in particular, the connectivity it brought. One of her last texts to Garbhán read: 'What Twitter signal do I press for Michelle O'Neill? [Deputy First Minister]. Please. Grá.'

Indeed, it never occurred to any of us that Áine would stop writing. She was such a prolific and gifted communicator. Just before she died, she had been working on a new draft of the story, included here, of how the family dog Schwarz (1980-1999) welcomed Úna to our family, and she was very keen to ensure we would have it included in the new print run of her book, ready for Christmas.

The letters, and emails, and poems, and texts are a real miss in our lives. If the phone ever buzzed before eight in the morning, it was invariably Áine, with a reminder of whatever celebration it was we had nearly forgotten. We are counting on her good friends, particularly those who know their Irish feast days, to continue with this particular tradition.

* * *

After the first edition of this memoir was published, Áine began revisiting her files to recover – and, occasionally, redo – stories we had missed. That work is included here in this new edition. Out of necessity, we decided, for the most part, to forgo Áine's massive pre-digital archive for now. Tracking down and editing seventy-plus years of handwritten letters and cards – not to mention her countless papers, articles and broadcast scripts (including her contributions to the BBC's Thought for the Day slot) will require a little more time.

We would like to thank all of those who helped us put together this 'continuum', including: Áine's surviving siblings Brigdín Conway (Killough) and Diarmaid Morton (Dublin); her sister-in-law Nuala Morton; her granddaughter Brónagh who had saved a mini-treasure trove of pre-digital poems; her great friend and mentor Fionnuala Geary for her memorial poem (reproduced here); Dr Nicola Duffy for the 'Your Derry' interview; and her neighbour Marie Dunne for ensuring we resurrected 'Torch in My Pocket'.

We also wish to express our deepest appreciation to hundreds of other friends, neighbours and family members who sent us cards, letters, messages and – crucially – memories in the weeks following Áine's death. Our mother had such a profound, positive influence on so many people, and will be remembered for her kindness, compassion and humour, every bit as much as for her wisdom and determination.

There will, very likely, be a second standalone volume of Áine's work at a later date, when we have a proper chance to compile the complete archive. But for the moment, we can all cherish some bonus time now, courtesy of an inspirational woman, who wrote beautifully gentle, fitting and thoughtful vignettes about her life and the world around her – and always left us wanting more.

Áine Downey (née Morton)
1942-2020
Déan coirnéal beag di

Read Me Like A Book

In pristine condition the unread book
Untouched by human hand, flat paged.
Like the virgin plaster statue
No worried frown to crease the purity.
There is no soul between the covers.

Becoming dishevelled the book that's read
Holding memory in, thumb held, curling pages.
Like the mother after birth
Blotchy, labour spoiled, complexion.
There is wonder between the covers.

Áine
February 1991

The Morton who pretended to read

The Mortons were an academic family. All six children availed of third-level education, as had their father Richie before them. Deirdre would became a leading light in the Queen's Celtic Department a decade before Áine would join the teaching staff at (what was then) Magee University College. At times, though, it was tough for the youngest child to keep up – even if Áine was destined to become the first of the siblings to be awarded a doctorate.

* * *

The expression 'letting down the family name' comes to mind when I think of education and our family. I don't have a memory of these words being used, in Irish or English, but the sensation was present at many critical times.

I do recall the presence of the sensation when, at school, ones were talking about what they would get if they passed the 11-Plus and that was the thought-sensation that crossed my mind if I didn't pass. Being the youngest of the six Mortons, when I was at that age, the three big ones – Deirdre, Diarmaid and Antoine – were at Queens: Celtic, Engineering and Mathematics. By the time I was eleven Deirdre was already employed as a research assistant in the Celtic Department, and this event was greeted as extremely educationally prestigious, an academic feather in the Morton cap.

So with Brigdín and Máire Róisín at Saint Dominic's [the girls grammar school on Belfast's Falls Road] well on the road to third-level education, it's clear that my mother's educational expectation for us three wee ones was high.

Back a step; as to whether my hiccups with education merited this potential of not quite being up to the Morton standard …well, unpredictable, is probably the most charitable description. The fact of being moved back from Senior Infants to Infants three times must have been a source of maternal concern. (That it never occurred to anyone that I was sent to school far too young, according to Brigdín us three all were. I was only three but in order to accommodate a second Catholic family who temporarily had moved into the street and had a daughter of the school starting age, and they were threatening to send her to the State/Protestant local school unless she had a companion in the class, I was the volunteer… in my memory her name was Ann Savage.)

Moving class didn't cause me any real distress, it was the same room, same teacher, three seats across, but unfamiliar story-books, and Senior Infants pointed to the squiggles on the page rather than talk to the picture. You see I didn't know what 'reading' was, there were books and I simply memorised the stories by the pictures, I was happily copying the actions and feeling quite pleased with myself. In fact, I was probably the best non-reader reader in the Infant class at getting through the available books, as I had an excellent memory, I had no concept of anything being wrong with this way of proceeding with books, so I had no idea why I was being switched desks nor why my poor mother was so upset.

But I well remember the day I CAUGHT reading – what a day that was!

I must have been clearing the table after tea and I lifted the squat rectangular milk jug advertising Coleraine whiskey.

"Why does this say 'Call Her Áine'?" says I.

I lifted a missal that was lying around, it fell open at a litany to Our Lady in Irish, no problem, I'd got it. The shapes on the page could connect with words coming out of my mouth. Magic.

Suddenly something clicked, everything made sense, and with it came the big realisation that I would no longer break my mother's heart.

* * *

Was that the end of my problems with this thing called education? No, not at all.

I caught reading, but the same could not be said about spelling (text spelling hadn't yet been invented), giving rise to the not-very-funny joke that I am 'illiterate in two languages'.

It really was the fact that the three big ones had set the bar so high that made our schooling so tricky for us three wee ones, but we did more than survive our parents' expectations and were very proud of Deirdre's growing expertise in spreading knowledge of Irish place-names.

I knew in my heart of hearts that studying subjects the others hadn't was the solution to this education comparison problem, but subject choice was limited. I nearly achieved the goal at advanced level, and at university I hit the jackpot: psychology through science. But it did take a phone call from Professor Seth to assure and reassure the parents that not studying Scholastic Philosophy alongside psychology would not have me excommunicated. Freedom to explore this extensive library unburdened.

* * *

I have this wee postscript, as soon as I knew that I had got a doctorate I phoned Mammy in Belfast. The line was engaged so I got Deirdre who lived up the street. I told Deirdre my news and she ran down to get whomever off the phone so I could tell Mammy. Dialled again. Says Mammy to me: 'Isn't it great, Áine? Deirdre got her doctorate.'

Grá

A torch in my pocket

I remember as a child writing out my address and finishing with Europe, Northern Hemisphere, The World, The Universe, little realising the influence of the light/dark of 'the northern hemisphere' in my life.

For most of my childhood I lived in Belfast with the main mod cons of 1940s, yet the highlights of my town life were visits to the Braniel to my aunties. This location of happiness had the mod cons of the turn of the century. Yes there was running water and an indoor toilet, however, one mile from the Belfast boundary, that was your lot!

Auntie Florrie was a dressmaker; show, or draw, her a picture of your dream dress or coat and she would cut the pattern out of newspaper and on her singer sewing machine a miracle would happen.

Josie was the reader and storyteller, sitting in the corner, listening to the radio, oh such a 1940s' wireless with the big red eye and this huge cold acid battery, which had to be lugged the mile down to the garage at the bus terminus to be recharged. She read the daily paper cover to cover and listened to all the client's stories, all these stories could get woven into a great night's entertainment.

Blanche cooked and baked the best shortbread in the world in the primus stove – gas and electricity, so readily available in the city, had yet to reach the Braniel.

Och, but I felt so safe there.

* * *

The early evening, after tea, was when the real pleasures of the day began. For this young townie the most popular entertainment was when there would be someone in getting fitted for clothes. There had to be a good fire on to heat the iron in case it was required, and Florrie's customers never came alone, there would be friends, sisters, mothers, and a neighbour or two would drop in. It was akin to the Irish story used to demonstrate how there was always room for another soul in heaven – a neighbour goes out of an evening looking for some place to céilí and at one of the houses there would be everyone crowded sitting round a turf fire, and s/he would say, "Déan coirnéal beag domh"(make a wee corner for me), and everyone would shuffle round a bit and there would appear a space where there was none before. "Sin mar a bheidh sé ar neamh" (that's how it will be in heaven), and a glimpse of heaven best describes those evenings.

And the conversations were varied, from the unsolved crossword clues to the travel books of HV Morton and, in my more adult life, Dervla Murphy, interspersed with comments and critical commentary on the state of the world and critical acclaim on the clothes that were being produced.

The other late-afternoon/early-evening ritual involved the tin can that held halfpennies and pennies being ceremonially lifted down from the shelf beside the wireless and an equal number of coins placed in a pile for each of the card players. Solo whist was the most popular game; a halfpenny for a simple solo, and tuppence for a misère.

At the end of the evening, perhaps seven o'clock, even eight as a special treat, the torch would be lifted off the hook at the back door and Florrie (or a neighbour) would walk me down the wee pathway to the 'green country bus' stop, which was located next to a deep ditch on the opposite side of the road.

Batteries and little torch bulbs played a central role in the Braniel life. No batteries? Well, I have told you about the lifeline of the radio, but the evenings were dark and, as well as getting safely to the bus stop, there was a 'river' outside the back door into which the tea leaves were ceremoniously emptied and it would have been very easy to miss your step, so the torch, and having a spare battery and bulb, were essentials.

* * *

It was the year after Santa brought me the doll with the china face that I asked for, and got, my very own first torch. And it was just as well, as my best friend, who lived in a farm about a mile out the road from the Braniel, and I had planned a song and dance routine that we were planning to bring round the neighbourhood as a kind of winter travelling entertainment. 'Put another nickel in' was one of the routines, and seventy years on I can still recall it. The nerve of us at seven years of age going from farmhouse to farmhouse and entertaining the natives! I don't recall any traffic, not even a bicycle on the roads that winter; we had the moon, the stars and our torches. We were not stupid and this travelling show did not perform in the wet weather; as long as it was dry we were immune to the cold, and we had light (mind you our guardian angels were kept on their toes that winter).

And thus began a lifelong relationship with the torch. Whether it was going to work in India or Nigeria, and especially going on holidays to Donegal, the torch, like the passport, got packed in the hand luggage. Goodness, the torches I have known, and the joy they have given me; from presenting a brother with a 'wind up' torch, so marking the end of our dependency on the battery, to the 'give it a few shakes' torch now making my life so simple.

* * *

In theory, living in Derry with all the innovations of the twenty-first century, the need for a torch should be non-existent. However the back lane, with the back doors of the big houses, between my wee safe house and the park is unlit and having this half-Labrador in long term foster care, well, the park is a bit of a necessity and an evening walk is part of the daily duties.

This corner, the cul-de-sac of the De Burghs – it's a bit of déjà vu, the combination of the neighbours evoke the feelings of the ease of Braniel early evenings.

We have the 'fixers', singers, dancers, entertainers, storytellers and chefs, and once or twice a year the women meet up in one of the houses, each of us bringing our 'savoury' or 'sweet' as well as the crack for the night. Yes, the occasions are more formal in that we sit round the table, yet, as different neighbours arrive, "déan coirnéal beag domh" is still the same, and a "coirnéal" appears for all.

At the end of the evening, now more like midnight than eight o'clock, I go to leave by the back door, "Are you okay for going down the back lane?"

"Sure, I've got a torch in my pocket."

Stay calm and keep baking

The scullery in Clara Street had the big sack of flour in the corner beside the back door. This sack was for quite some time the hiding place for the rationed butter until Antoine 'The Butter Finder' located it.

I have no memory of anyone lugging the sack into the house, but it was always there and essential for the baking of Mammy's bread and the pastry for the apple tarts and meat pies. But my absolute favourite, especially on a cold winters evening, was the spud apple. This was a 'waste not want not' dish (I look to Brigdín to correct me): it was like a pastry of leftover potatoes mashed with the flour and Echo Margarine (pretend butter); the topping was cooking apples and brown sugar (was there syrup in the topping?); into the oven and in less than half an hour a sticky, sweet, gooey spud apple emerged, perfect for Halloween or Sunday visitors.

While homemade soda bread fried in bacon fat was definitely a treat, it was a frequent feast and as such it doesn't count: so it was the 'variations' from the bakery which came via the bread van that were regarded as treats. The batch loaves, still warm, stuck together in the broad middle drawers of the van, and you broke off the required number. The smell, the joyful anticipation of pulling the warm, outer strips of bread – no need for butter and never to be insulted with the dreaded margarine; the modern, wrapped batch version is bereft of this treat.

The loaf itself was at its next best when a slice was carefully balanced on the prongs of the big fork (there was a proper toasting fork in the Braniel) and toasted in front of the fire. There was an expertise to this task, getting the exact degree of toasting without burning the toast; not letting the bread fall into the fire; and not burning your fingers. I always tried to find a scrape of butter for this delicacy but sometimes had to resort to the dreaded Echo.

The finger licking of the butter icing of Máire Róisín's sponge cake was both a delicacy and an acquired skill. How butter icing? Either rationing of the butter had ended or there had been butter smuggled from over the border. Regardless, the butter and icing-sugar mix between the two sponges was plentiful and delicious.

The trick for the baker was to squeeze the two sponges together so as to have an overflow for the extended middle finger of the right hand to scoop; after licking this delicious morsel you flattened the top sponge to try to cover up the evidence. It was difficult in a family of six children to have more than a smidgen of the butter icing left by the time the cake was to be eaten! Betty Crocker's is good but it isn't in the same league as Máire's.

The bread van sometimes contained donkeys lugs in the bottom drawer – a circle/round of eight ear-shaped sweet bread covered with thick, just-about-set, white icing, I have no memory of any other bread-van sweet bread.

When we moved to nearer the Ormeau Bakery and rationing was no more, it was the barmbrack* toasted on the cooker grill (the brack was too heavy for the open fire toasting), oozing with melted real butter that became a breakfast treat. The full range of breads, sweet breads and buns are now available in the corner shop and the bread van calling at your home is no more.

Le grá

[*Also spelt 'barnbrack', a fruit loaf, popular in Belfast.]

The Glasgow wake

The memory-picture image of the Clara Street kitchen focuses on the importance of the fireplace in the wall facing the scullery door, with the table that could seat maybe six against the parlour wall facing the window to the yard.

Houses had kitchens, sculleries and parlours. Now it wasn't just that the parlour was the good room kept for important visitors, it really was a no-no area for children except for 'punishment' homework, but because we had a pedal organ in the parlour we occasionally snuck in to pretend we were musicians. The wind-up gramophone normally lived in the parlour along with the precious '78' records, being kept relatively safe from prying small people.

Most visitors were entertained in the kitchen but for the important ones, like Mammy and Daddy McCann, a fire was lit in the parlour. I have a memory, crouched in the nook of the stairs (about two steps up) listening to the records and particularly interested in 'Little Bridget Flynn'. This record caused major consternation when Daddy brought it home from Smithfield, it seems some of the lyrics were shocking and were for adult ears only. From my curled up position I always thought 'I'd love to have her sitting on my knee' was the offending lyric, however Diarmaid knows the significant offensive ditty that was an addendum to Little Bridget.

Mammy's Donegal relatives returning by boat from

England for their holidays stopped off in Clara Street for breakfast in the kitchen. The big clue to their visits was being sent the day before to walk down the town to Gilroy's shop in Ann Street for sausages; these were celebration breakfasts with the McHughs, Seamus, Annie or Kitty and her daughter (Anne) with beautiful red hair; these were times when the atmosphere was of laughter, hope and joy.

But this day felt very different. Somewhere in my pre-memory I must have absorbed the celebratory atmosphere, perhaps that's why this is such a strong memory, I have always regarded this occasion as the first memory I have.

I can see Mammy sitting to the right of the fireplace and her foot on the wee side metal holder that kept the teapot warm. For reasons, unknown to me then, the three big ones were between the scullery and the back yard seemingly interested in playing with us three wee ones. Occasionally one or other of them would unwillingly disappear in to the kitchen and quickly re-emerge; as they were going in I would juke through the door and there were two men sitting on the other side of the fire place. Eventually it was my turn to be called. Without doubt I loved to show off; singing and dancing were always my specialty even at this tender age of about three.

My mother gobsmacked me, really stopped me in my wee tracks; says Biddie Pheadar Mháire: "Seo Áine, níl sise faiteach." ["This is Aine, she's not shy."] I have a vague memory of singing but it was (my child interpretation) the unhappy atmosphere of the occasion that stuck. This was the occasion of the youngest of her family, Paddy, emigrating to Glasgow from their home in Donegal, and the tradition was to have a leaving party, the Glasgow Wake. I realise now that Mammy called each of us in turn to perform a 'party piece'.

It was twenty-ish years later, after Uncle Niall (of November 2nd prayers' fame) died here in Derry, and I was going through the letters he had kept and writing to each person to let them know of his death, that I came across Paddy's address in Glasgow.

I was delighted when his son Peter came to stay with us for a few days, it was like completing a memory circle: we gave Peter a truly memorable leaving party.

Ad Majorem Dei Gloriam

"Profess your faith openly/Never deny your religion' was the mantra of the Northern, well definitely Belfast, Catholic in the 40s and 50s.

'Are they one of us' was the Mammy whisper when meeting a stranger. We were obsessed with national identity and religious affiliation when growing up. As soon as a front door was opened you knew the religion of the incumbents; Catholics had a mini holy-water font at the door so as you could bless yourself on entering and leaving. In case you missed this first clue, as soon as you went into the kitchen/living room, there hanging in the middle of the brace wall over the fireplace with eyes that followed you round the room was the framed picture of the Sacred Heart; and the more wealthy Catholics had a little red electric light crucifix just underneath. Other holy pictures that I prayed to when they set fire to the City Dump at the back of our Clara Street house were Our Lady of Perpetual Succour, The Holy Family, agus Babaí Íosa.

It wasn't really that I had a favourite, it was more that I operated on a results system, and Our Lady of Perpetual Succour never once let me down or let our house catch fire.

The evening Rosary in Irish, regardless of the religion or language of those present, took place at half past six. Just five simple decades; there was no escape but at least we didn't indulge in trimmings.

At school at the top of each and every jotter page

and good exercise book page I wrote 'Pro Deo', and so all schoolwork was a tribute to God and his one true church, and God was definitely masculine. In case you might forget any of this, at least once a year there was the school retreat dominated by holy pictures, sins of impurity and silence. My favourite holy picture was The Good Shepherd. As adolescent girls we sent each other these pictures and your missals held the evidence of your popularity.

It was Derry that was promoting the statue of the Infant Child of Prague – and still has the tradition of putting the statue outdoors on the eve of a wedding to ensure good weather. As an adopted Derry-person, I visited the original and was impressed by the range of the Infant's delicate 'outfits'. Otherwise, as far as I was concerned, my days of being surrounded by religious imagery were in the past – until…

There were/are two 'Holy' shops in Waterloo Street, Derry and, when I was in my late 40s, at Laoise Flanagan's insistence, we walked up and down spending considerable time staring at the images in the windows – until Laoise confessed that at one specific/particular angle you could get the Sacred Heart to blink!

And then 20-ish years ago Ruby's icon entered my life.

A friend, Father John, used to spend his months holiday to give relief to a priest who administered to the men on death row in one of the American prisons. It was at a fundraising event over there to provide the men with money for reading glasses and other essentials, that Ruby donated the Icon of Our Lady of Perpetual Succour that her grandmother had brought with her when emigrating to the USA from Russia.

John told me he was leaving it to me in his will but then decided my need was immediate and greater than his and so Ruby's grandmother's treasured Icon came from Russia to Derry to have pride of place in my home, initially with Waterford glass candlesticks and proper Termonbacca wax candles, one on each side.

However, fifteen years ago Scruffy, a very nearly labrador belonging to Garbhán, Úna and the Derry grandchildren, entered my life and with one swipe of the wagging tail, the Waterford glass had to be replaced, firstly by ordinary glass candlesticks and, most recently, by small squat glass/plastic candle sticks. So damage is now limited to singed dog-tail-hair.

And to complete the circle, about three years ago Cecelia, (Úna's mother) gifted me a holy water font for the front door and rosary beads from Medjugorje.

I have no choice in this matter – I might not be professing, but there's no denying my religion.

Grá

Taibhdhearc Bhéal Feirste

I suppose you had to be socially enterprising when you were a proud Irish-speaking Catholic in the Belfast of the Fifties and wanted to meet the opposite sex – legitimately and cheaply. Diarmaid Morton and two friends Dioraí Ó Corbáin and Len Quigley were inspired – their solution – an Irish Drama group, to my knowledge a first for Belfast.

The stage of the Ard Scoil at the foot of the Falls Road was used for the performances; a rented rehearsal room in Royal Avenue in the centre of the city. Those were three young men whose intentions were…no different to the intentions of the18-year-old male. Other like-minded people, especially young women looking to socialise, seemingly paid a membership fee and this covered the rents.

I wasn't needed to act in any of their plays but poor Deirdre, whom I assume was an honorary member, was frequently substituted at the last moment in many of their productions: Mammy and us three wee ones were required for, and at times to be exclusively, the audience.

Nuala, whom Diarmaid married, didn't have Irish and was the backstage holder of the torch, whereas Ethna Warren, who later married Len, presented with aspirations to having enough Irish, wished to be selected for leading roles.

Friends of Deirdre's from Queen's An Cumann Gaelach were frequently given non-starring roles, however, following the dress rehearsal Deirdre was invariably handed the female lead part to learn for the next night. These were her pre-Vespa days and I have an image of her sitting on the bus travelling down the Ormeau Road on her way to Queen's, script in hand.

The year of A Midsummer Nights Dream (the translation was mostly combined membership Royal Avenue work), however, the big back yard was required to make costumes. I used to sit in the drink-delivery lorry and watch.

Bottom's costume presented great problems for the three engineers. But in my memory this was the summer of the singing; the motley crew translated songs into Irish and practiced while inventing the props and costumes. The only one I still remember is The Sash: 'Bhí se sean, is bhí sé deas go leor.' Even at seven or eight years of age, I sensed it was one-upmanship and naturally practiced while sitting in the lorry pretending to drive.

Before Taibhdhearc Bhéal Feirste the most embarrassing Morton experiences in my life related to daddy and buses; when asked to produce the ticket for the inspector he would give a mathematical formula for our stop number, e.g. seventeen cubed plus five to the power of six, nightmare. However, even more embarrassing were the occasions when we had to stand in the trolley-bus or tram holding onto the rail; the loud clear of the throat and at the top of his voice, "Do not forsake me oh my darlin'." High Noon had a lot to answer for.

These instances disappear into the ether when compared to the very first performance in front of Belfast gaeilgeoirí. In this never-to-be-forgotten debut, the play was a husband and wife story: who the original female lead was I do not recall but for the opening night it was Diarmaid and, word perfect, Deirdre. The tension was building as the wife was realising the husband's 'away days' coincided with public hangings, and there was much handwringing and pacing up and down... In comes the husband from his secret work with a gift of a pearl necklace and (mental drumroll) goes to place it round her neck. Dramatic and traumatic was the look of terror on Deirdre's face as he was fixing the clasp, and yes it happened, the string broke and in slow motion one by one each pearl dropped, not into her lap, onto the stage and with the energy from the break and with unerring accuracy each pea clattered off the stage into the audience... each time either of them went to speak the next line, the movement activated another pearl. While Diarmaid and Deirdre kept their composure, we – the audience – did not.

In recognition of the memory of this significant event in our lives, the Morton girls could never again wear pearl necklaces – no matter how fashionable.

[* Footnote from Wikipedia: 'The word *taibhdhearc* appears as a gloss for the Latin *teatrum* (theatre) in an old Irish document, derived from roots meaning "dream" and "glance". The modern Irish for a theatre is *amharclann*.']

Letter to Rónán

Rónán was born in January 1968 and died in December 2000, almost 20 years before his mother. There is no date on the original hand-written letter from Áine.

You made your presence known from Day 1. One look in the bathroom mirror declared that the 'dry boaks' was not a hangover but a major life event. The pregnancy test simply confirmed what the morning people already knew. Did you know Garbhán had been there before you? Did you smell him? I remember thinking that the first home would be more welcoming for you; fewer jagged edges.

I had what was called an 'ESN' fourth-year class, and they were both streetwise and very caring. I can still see Mary F. following me around with a chair and telling me that I had to sit down and rest myself – yes that 4E were determined that this would be a stress-free time and, of course, while they were taking care of me, how could I shout at them? And they were much more interested in my life than in their schooling. It was pregnancy and child development (Garbhán's) as the core curriculum.

I was making friends with a number of the teachers; Maureen Hunt and Jean Flaherty and I had met, and I was starting to get to know Gemma and Joan. The lost feeling was gone, I seemed to be more at myself now in Derry, and you seemed very content, settled and enjoying of adult company. Riversdale Road was a welcoming place for people to call. And on Saturday night's it was [everybody] back to the house for homemade soup and home brew.

Your first trip to Magee, you must have been twelve-ish weeks, was for me to be "talked to" (theoretically interviewed) for part-time lecturing in Psychology – as there was no one else. Needless to say, I got the job. I must admit though, I played down how chuffed I was in front of Gerry; with you I was the fella in the big picture and told you how great I was. And so you were introduced to the Magee Senior Common Room, Trinity College, and all the accompanying trappings.

There was a sadness in me, too. I was losing touch with brothers and sisters and would talk a lot to you and Garbhán about my fears. Mammy was busy with Brigdín and Pat, and it seem to me that Brigdín had it made, while I was juggling with the home and now two jobs, one of which I didn't even bother to tell them about. But there was something else now that I couldn't understand, a distancing with Deirdre and Diarmaid, and virtually no communication with Máire Róisín and Antoine. And so, while the Downeys were preparing for Angela's wedding, I was feeling very isolated from the Mortons and I can only assume that my fierce need to protect myself – I didn't seem to belong to an original family – flowed through you too. I told you about keeping up a front and never to let the world see any vulnerability and cried a lot when Garbhán was in bed and we were alone.

Though I had maternity leave from St Mary's, I

didn't have from Magee, but there was plenty of time for you and Garbhán and me to go around the shops, and I was so proud of myself with a toddler in one hand and this enormous bump (you're in the film of Angela's wedding) for all the world to see, and me with the oh-so-important job.

Angela and Mickey were with us, and I had some marking to do for the beginning of term when I started to bleed and was driven over to Altnagelvin, into a little ward of my own, oh yes, you were going to arrive in style – I think this was the first time I really realised how elitist and deferential Derry was. And yes, it was frightening that you were going to arrive your way, taking a long time and with afterbirth first.

I think I know you better now.

Home brew

Pat Conway loved to be ahead, and at the head, of the posse and Brigdín Morton had her choice of men – so, poor Sean G (who could have been regarded a good catch) hadn't a chance.

Pat was a doer; the hunting and fishing I first saw when they were on the Glencolmcille holidays, but Pat came into his own when they moved to Killough.

It was still the tradition in the more rural areas of Ireland that the school principal was central to life in the villages, and Pat really loved being principal of the school and his leadership involvement with the whole community. It wasn't just that he did this so well, he really cherished the position and gave it his all. Undoubtedly, the house Brigdín and Pat chose and eventually secured is the best in the village, however, they used it to the full – seldom has a (former) rectory known such energy, vitality and activity. Coupled with all this, Pat was easy to like, affable, he loved people and, for the most part, saw the good in people. And both himself and Brigdín were hospitable people.

While Pat and Brigdín lived in South Parade with the parents, on a Thursday he would join Daddy and Mr Murphy in Lavery's Bar and needless to say got to know their hosts. And when, a few years later, these same Laverys procured the franchise for 'Home Brew', not only did they inform Pat immediately, but he was in like a shot!

* * *

Pat wholeheartedly embraced his enthusiasms, Brigdín and their daughters, his work, his friendships, as well as the more rural way of life. It was when they lived in Earlswood Road that the beer and winemaking was all the rage. Pat with his wonderful customary exuberance bought all the equipment: a fermentation tank, demijohns, bungs and corks, lots of tubing, airlock caps, grommets and much more besides. He then proceeded to take over all the space in the kitchen that wasn't required for 'normal' daily living. Mammy still making bread, Brigdín (teaching locally in Ballyhackamore) doing the cooking, and a woman, her name escapes me, whose sparkling clean windows were a joy to behold.

* * *

Introduce into this scenario two extremely curious Derry boys who loved to visit Neanaí, play with the cousins and their toys, and generally enthusiastically distribute excess energy after a two-hour confined car journey. This is the same Garbhán and Rónán who one early morning proudly, and excitedly, exploded into the bedroom covered in soot. They had been 'helping' by cleaning the chimney. When 'quietly and gently' enquiring as to why, we were told, 'You never told us not to.'

Brigdín and Pat were great hosts and, now well fed and watered, while relaxing and discussing world affairs in general and Morton family affairs in particular, Pat took the children off through the kitchen to the back of the house and kept them entertained.

I have this photograph, a memory-image in my head of the kitchen countertop that day; two, possibly three demijohns with brown corks/bungs connected by a complicated array of plastic tubing; it was an impressive, even professional looking, display of 'brewer at work' – Pat took his recreational activities very seriously.

* * *

Back home, how did I not notice the boys eyeing-up/ showing interest in such home-brewing kit as we had? It was when I found them, with our two demijohns (bunged and corked), connected up with some plastic tubing, wielding the potato peeler that the penny dropped, and I had to tell a nine-year-old and a seven-year-old: "You are NOT making poteen, no matter what Pat Conway is doing."

Nowadays they could learn from 'You Tube' but I think learning from Pat Conway was much more exciting.

Le grá

Letter from Maya Angelou

When Áine first showed us this letter, more than thirty years ago, only Rónán grasped its significance. This was six years before her pen pal had delivered the inaugural, Grammy-winning recitation at Bill Clinton's installation as US president. Fiachra later studied Maya Angelou for A Level, and Áine rediscovered this letter, which he was then able to cite in an assignment. There is, unfortunately, no remaining copy of the letter Áine sent to the poetess.

Z. Smith Reynolds Professor of American Studies
Wake Forest University
Drawer 7229 Reynolds Station
Winston-Salem
North Carolina 27109

Dec 29, '87

Dear Áine Downey, (hope the spelling is correct)

Your letter is a glittering gem. A present, a gift of lucidity during a murky season. How, when in the name of Christ, we buy and sell, give and receive shoddily made items and bawl "Merry Xmas" (the X is supposed to eradicate Christ from the negotiations) I had need of a simply beautiful gift. Thank you for sending it to me from Derry.

Áine, I think all women, all thinking, feeling courageous women, are war-weary. We are a gender under siege, whether in Derry, Palestine, Alabama, Johannesburg, Beirut, Manila or in our home living rooms and beds. I am certain that we will survive and by our survival save the species. Not merely save its physical aspects but preserve our gentleness, our wit, our mercy, our courage, our faith and our gorgeous humor. We must not surrender any part of that list, in fact we must discover in our humanness more, and list more and cherish more.

I hope the students have been gratifying. What do you teach?

Write soon please. What books would you like? I'd be pleased to send you loads. And I do hope to come to Ireland.

I wish you and yours a splendid New Year.

Joy!

Maya Angelou

Women and Easter
(Translation from Irish, April 1988)

From Palm Sunday until Easter Sunday, I feel very sad and extremely guilty. I spend my time thinking of:

- the Judas in me
- the Pontius Pilate in me, and
- the Peter in my being.

And I would prefer simply to go to bed for the week and pull the blankets over my head. To tell the truth, I'm in no form to celebrate anything – even the Resurrection. I'm feeling so awful and so guilty, and that's not like me at all.

But something wonderful happened this year. There came to me a significant understanding that transformed my outlook, and from this Easter on my life is totally changed.

It happened like this; have I told you before that this woman has severe difficulties with the Church of Christ, with the practices of these churches at this time, in this country? At the beginning and end of the story, the greatest difficulty I have is that I am woman, with the body of woman, the nature of woman and the spirit of woman and most of the time I feel that these churches are telling me that my body, my nature, my spirit is not in the Image of God.

Consequently, this Lent, and particularly during Passion Week, I spent my time reading about the women in the Gospels and thinking about the kind of lives they led.

The Feast of the Passover, the most important feast of the year – just like our Christmas and we all know how busy all the woman are in the days leading up to Christmas – and remember there was no fridge-freezer in the kitchen two thousand years ago. Reflect on the foods of the Passover, the lamb, the unleavened bread, the sauces of herbs and spices, and if the families of the women of Jerusalem were anything like mine, these women would also have to be cooking the normal daily meals.

So, on the Wednesday and Thursday, the women of Jerusalem were cleaning their houses, washing the clothes, finishing knitting the new jumpers and cooking. They didn't have much time, nor were they in any frame of mind, to go to any person's trial.

And on the Friday, and the women out doing the last-minute shopping, remember the shops were going to be closed for a few days, what happened? They stopped in their tracks, they stared at Christ and they started to cry. And these women were crying so deeply that Christ noticed them and stopped on this last journey to speak to them – the women of Jerusalem who didn't know Christ, they were crying. I'm feeling a little bit better now that I am woman.

And what about the women who did know Christ? Well, I suppose you would expect the mother to remain by him – but what about that magnificent, proud Mary Magdalen? Did she say, 'No, I don't know him'? No way!

We only have two other names of women, Salome and Mary, but as well as that there is one line written 'there were a lot of women there that followed Christ from Galilee.' Wow – I'm feeling proud that I am woman.

And as soon as the feast of the Passover was finished – first thing in the morning, who went to the tomb? Three women.

Only now can this woman celebrate the Resurrection.

But next year, when we are reading Christ's Passion and when the congregation are asked to read the part of the public two thousand years ago – i.e. to chant 'Crucify him, crucify him', I like to think that I will stick my hand in the air – 'Excuse me,' I'll say, 'but the women of Galilee were following Christ.' I know I haven't that kind of courage but maybe, just maybe, one of you readers will.

Notes from a book launch

Áine was asked to give the keynote speech at the launch of the Foyle Hospice legacy book, Building Bridges, in December 2005. Rónán had been a patient at the hospice in 2000, and Áine then served as a volunteer at the hospice until 2017 when she was no longer fit for a three-hour stand in the kitchen. Rónán's experiences, attempting to negotiate the health services prior to availing of the hospice, inspired Áine to become a director of the Western Health Board and the organisation's Complaints' Convenor.

Go mbeannaí Dia daoibh uilig. Good evening everyone.

It is timely that the story of the Foyle Hospice is being told – this time between the two 'comings of age', more than 18 and not yet 21. [The hospice was founded in 1985.]

And the spirit of this time selected Dr Keith Munro, whose longstanding commitment to the hospice is known and appreciated by all – so it was Dr Keith who was chosen to volunteer to author the story.

No this wee country is very partial to its myths and legends – for example last week there wasn't a stadium large enough to host all the people who insisted they witnessed George Best, single-handed, take on the Scotland soccer team. And the Foyle Hospice story is not immune to the 'I was there when Dr Tom [McGinley, the hospice founder] said...' or 'I was there when the architects talked about putting in an extra window, and so Dr Keith had the unenviable task of separating myth and legend from the story and, given some of the fantastic and bizarre episodes described, you are sometimes left wondering…

Dr Keith tells a story of love: the love of a community in the northwest margin of Ireland and the love in the community; and he does this by permitting this story of love to be told through him; a rare gift, to listen well, to hear well.

The love of family shines through this story; the love in the McIntyre family and how their love drove Angela to influence the hospice story in a very powerful manner.

Agus scéal pearsanta chlann McGinley, an grá idir Deirdre (d. 2003) agus Tom agus iomlan an chlann – tá mé buíoch go bhfuil grianghraf den chlann uilig ar leathanach dhá chéad is a naoi. This story is movingly told in the chapter 'Dispatches from the Heart'.

The love of a community wanting to help each other through difficult times is told through the stories of the Hospice Support Group.

Dr Keith tells the stories of the symbolism of the love – the choice of the Bridge symbol, the choice of the two children to perform the official opening – these are powerful stories.

Each of you will find your own favourite story of love in this northwestern community, but for me it is on page 45, the first line: 'Fundraising had been curtailed during the Ethiopian famine crisis during 1985…'

*　*　*

This is a story of deep emotions and Dr Keith describes the personal emotions and the statutory authorities' 'emotions' in a dramatic yet understated way.

The personalities in this story, they're no shrinking violets and I would have loved to have been a fly on the wall when some of the head-to-heads between the committee and the non-funders were taking place.

However, it is the emotional reactions of the statutory authorities that fascinated me. There were two pearls of wisdom missing in the experiences and knowledge of the Department of Health and the Western Health and Social Services Board (prior to my involvement).

Firstly, why did they not appreciate that this was not just any community but the community of the northwest margin of Ireland which is itself on the margin of Europe. We all know the importance of the margin – take out your jotter, ruler and pencil and rule out the margin. The most creative work is done in the margin and then a small, tidy piece of this work is brought to the centre of the page to the teacher-slash-authority. And the authorities did not have the eyes to see or the wit to know the hundreds if not thousands of people working creatively in the margins.

Dr Keith reminds us that their reaction was the full force of historical inertia [no way] and then the sneaky, sneaky offer of a totally unsuitable site in an attempt to save face.

Now, the second pearl of wisdom unknown to the statutory authorities and here I quote a friend of ours, John Murtagh: 'The Irishman's gift is not for invention but for brilliant improvisation.'

* * *

Dr Keith tells the story of both the spirit of the Foyle Hospice and also how spirituality resides at the heart of all its work.

While it is relatively easy for the person with a spiritual belief in the Rosary to see the Joy of love interacting with the Sorrow of terminal illness becoming transformed into the glory of the Foyle Hospice, the inter-faith nature of hospice spirituality is also powerfully Baha'i, Dr Keith's own spirituality.

* * *

Just in case that all I have referred to so far has not lured you into buying this history – in keeping with the Foyle Hospice tradition of inclusivity, maximum publicity and value for money in fundraising – Dr Keith has included a picture gallery.

And if you are not in any of the pictures in this book and, after this evening, you want to create your own Foyle Hospice myth or legend, you'd better have the evidence!

Serendipity

I must have been in my forties before I realised that coincidence did not occur by chance. I seem to have been quite slow to learn some of life's truths. And so, when the 'Please Do Not Shoot The Messenger' email arrived in October '05 that had the potential to establish or re-establish contact with Uncle Niall's daughter and granddaughter, and families in Brisbane, Queensland, I wasn't anticipating any coincidence.

I think it was Diarmaid and Nuala who sent me a piece from the paper of this family looking for anyone who knew of their father/grandfather and, in true Morton fashion, I was assigned the task. I recalled that Niall had given me a photograph of himself, taken in Drung, Redcastle, Donegal in 1963, with his daughter and two grandchildren. The memories of those few short months in 1964 to 1965 came flooding back, with the consequence that I was delighted to write to the address given in the paper – via a simple postcard of Derry – telling that I knew Niall and giving my address and e-address, and it was now up to the Queensland relatives as to whether or not they really did want to be in contact.

Well the contact came quickly and, in all forms of communication: email, letter and phone, a big warm family with the long McDermott backs, thirsting for knowledge of their Irish ancestry.

It's hard for the likes of me to comprehend this yearning for knowledge of your roots. Family folklore, most of it of the skeletons in the cupboard variety, was bread and butter to me [or maybe that should be 'bread and margarine'] when growing up, and I could have done without the half of it – yet here I was double-checking some of the stories with other family members and discovering the variations in our memories.

* * *

It must have been November when the 'macular hole' in the right eye announced its presence, and while I did thank God for sixty-three years of sight with both eyes and realised that a person can adapt to seeing the world with one eye, I did want to have the operation sooner rather than later and definitely sooner than the National Health Service would have me having it. And so I was sidelined from following through on the McDermott-Queensland connection like the bull in a china shop [which, in truth, is my usual style] in to researching postoperative care for macular hole surgery. Now, I was single minded in this task and any of you who wish to know about the actual surgery can look it up for yourselves – as far as I was concerned, the surgeon needed to know about the operation and I needed to know about the aftercare, and it was good to be in contact with the new-found relatives in Brisbane.

* * *

So Christmas came, and the depth of this longing for family really came home to me with the 'Now that I have found my Irish family, there is nothing more I want. Hey, all I did was reply to a letter in the paper,

And now the quest was to get the documentation needed for an Irish passport.

It was January, I now knew the operation was to be February 10, and I had made one of my mother's famous meat pies for a lunch with friends when Gay arrived and sat with us for a wee bite.

Garbhán, the eldest son, called to say hello and out of the blue, says Gay 'What do you think about 'us' doing the Derry heat of the Rose of Tralee?' I think she wanted to hear from Garbhán that this was a worthwhile event to be involved with, as it seems I was to be a member of the small backing group.

I am a good backing group, perhaps a bit loud and obvious [like in 'Tie a yellow ribbon round the old oak tree'], but effective, and was sure – given the operation and the recuperation time – doing this would shorten the winter.

* * *

So between the macular hole recovery, the Rose events, and the odd bits and pieces that occupy my daily life, I did search in all the usual places for the Uncle Niall photograph, to no avail. And when the Derry Rose got through to the 'To Be Televised' final, I probably did say that, yes, maybe I would go to the finals in Tralee in August provided we were all going.

* * *

We were starting to get to know each other this family in Brisbane Queensland and the Derry McDermott/Morton/Downey family, still a bit at arms length as you would expect, however, it was starting to look as if a visit to Ireland might be on the cards.

It was July when there was to be the neighbours' Irish-Welsh wedding, and the Number Cards for the wedding reception tables were to be in Irish and Welsh. Now, I did not have the old Irish script in the computer and with the help of friends located the site for the download.

Naturally all the instructions were in Irish and, sitting with Aoife, the computer buff, translating the information and her saying, "What's the Irish for 'download'?" And I reached up for the English-Irish dictionary on the shelf, and there inside the front cover was the photograph.

Yes we did the download, and then scanned in the photo and sent it round the world. The joy of finding the photo in these circumstances connected us all to the wedding story.

* * *

We did go to Kerry for the finals of the 2006 Rose of Tralee, not quite the predicted people, yet absolutely the right people. Now it is difficult to believe that this event in its 48th year had not anticipated where the television cameras needed to be in relation to the seating arrangements, needless to say we were 'displaced persons'.

We were relocated to the fourth row, fairly central, immediately behind the escorts – quite simply the best audience seats in the house.

The tradition is, seemingly, that before the final announcement, the escorts remove themselves and line up the centre of the hall, so that is how we had the full unimpeded view of the 30 Roses from all over the world, from Derry to Australia via America when the winner was announced.

The 2006 Rose of Tralee, the 48th Rose of Tralee, then came the drum roll for – Kathryn, The Queensland Rose.

As for me, I had forgotten that coincidence does not occur by chance and I hadn't placed a bet.

Grá

Notes from Nigeria

In early 2010, Áine visited Nigeria as part of a British Council delegation to establish educational/civic partnerships. She kept a handwritten account of her time there, though only some sections of this survive.

KANO

Being met at the airport and participating in the bureaucratic process of entering Nigeria for the first time makes the security process at Derry city seem extremely slipshod.

The British Council people met us as soon as we were through this particular stage of the shambolic activity and, on receiving our bags, ensured that we did not have to go through the activity of each bag being individually searched as was happening to the rest of the newcomers.

The form we had to complete with all our visa details etc. had at least been given to us on the flight and so was filled in in the relative comfort of a cramped airplane seat. The white form for first-time visitors was saved until we had landed and were in the queue for passport control. So there I was, hand luggage, handbag, passport with visa and general entry form standing in a queue in Kano airport [comparisons to City of Derry Airport would have CDA as luxurious] and being handed this A4 sheet of white paper to fill in with the same information as on the general-entry blue filled-in sheet, at 11.30 at night on a day that had begun at 3.15am. Undaunted, nothing ventured, nothing gained – without dropping my tenuous hold on the assorted belongings [never mind reality], I struggled womanfully to locate a pen and complete the form leaning on the ever so slightly inadequate surface size of the passport.

To get an official to take all of the necessary entry items was the next step. Not easy peasy. It takes three officials: one for the white form, one for the passport and blue form, and a third to check/coordinate the activities. Is that all, I hear you ask, not at all – then comes the double check – all clearances by one set of officials have to be checked by the other set of officials. So there was a great sense of relief that, after much discussion and loud-voices-type talking, we were eventually ushered through customs.

Our host had arranged supper and tea for us at the hotels and obviously had the expectation of collegiality after giving us thirty minutes to 'freshen up'.

And so it came to pass that in the early hours of the Sunday morning, we were to be found eating savoury Nigerian snacks and drinking tea/hot water and enthusiastically discussing how appreciative we were to be here, and eventually armed with bottles of cold water off to bed.

* * *

The problem with being an early riser is that I was awake at seven-ish, Nigerian time, and having kind of showered decided to go to see if there was Mass. I suspect that independence for the traveller is a no-no. However, as no one else of the group, or the two facilitators who are living in the hotel too, was up, off I go to the hotel manager to ask about church services. Extremely helpful he was and, having given me two fifty-something notes for collections sent me with one of the hotel cars to the Church of the Holy Cross. Picture the scene, it's about 8.20am the big foreboding high grey gates are locked and crowds of colourfully dressed, beautifully-clad women, children, men, hundreds of them, are gathered outside. Luckily, the driver had the wit to ask one of them for a return time.

I had been thinking of a quick nip-in for an impromptu 'thank God for a safe arrival and take care of the family until I return'-type visit, but 'twas not to be. The gates opened about 8.25am and we were ushered in, literally, by official ushers. I had hung back a bit and observed when entering the main body, lots of outside benches, 'the crying chapel' (?), noticed the men on the far side, the women and children on the near side, and it was choc-a-bloc. There was much shuffling and very kindly a space was found for me at the edge of a bench.

Meanwhile, the singing which was accompanying the entrance was joyous, loud, to dance to, and every one presented as extremely delighted to be there. There were offertory gifts, donations, and a procession of each row at a time joining the queue to present contributions at the front of the altar. The joyful singing for this procession was surpassed by the dancy, loud, clappy, musical, happy celebration (of the gifts) that followed; around the church and outside they danced, or simply stood up and sway-danced where you were.

It was the next two collections, accompanied by almost hypnotic song, that kind of disturbed me and left me wondering: one collection was for tithes and the next was for donations for intentions for the priest/s to bring to their visit to Rome.

This was followed by the Consecration and 'twas 10.00am and time for me to leave for the hotel car, through locked gates, opened specially for me and ones outside were not permitted in to the church. As I departed the children and the people in the processions stopped to shake my hand.

* * *

Sunday and we were given expenses, a SIM card [my wee mobile would not accept this] and you have to be struck at how well organised the BC facilitators are. Ola Ambassador Ladie, and Ramota and Omar seem to be staying here too, and Ola appears to be in charge of ensuring that all the arrangements are satisfactory.

The shopping [without the armed guard!!!!!] was a great success, lots of material bought for the tailor to measure us up for kaftans or whatever at 7.00pm.

Overall impression is of warm welcome and extremely well organised, no expense spared! Got two mosquito bites and they are, despite all the potions, going to be lulus.

* * *

Monday and the meeting with Ben Fisher (British Council) and the Kano Active Citizens. Okay, so being called at 7.00am for breakfast at 7.30am to start work at 8.30am was grand and the wearing of the Active Citizens T shirts and baseball caps was important for our hosts in relation to common identity. Seemed unusual for me, but sometimes it's good to go with the flow.

Some learnings to be thought about: "How we are presented is not who or how we really are" [Fatima]; also, the understanding of how being democratic means meeting your responsibilities to the minorities. There was a lengthy discussion on Nigerian identity; at one level for our education and, at another level, our presence proved to be a necessary catalyst for our hosts; interesting. This is an extremely well-resourced programme. While there is a limit on the total spending for projects, the budget for the cultural exchange aspects seems fulsome. [There is something about joining a group and group identity in relation to how people change – check Mari Fitzduff's thesis on people changing. And given that the only person I can change is myself, I think that this needs looking at.] Oíche mhaith.

It's the morning of March 4th, Garbhán and Úna's anniversary, and although I have two days to write up about, I'm starting with the early morning dreaming to the musical accompaniment of the second call to prayer and anticipating the fourteen mins of loud prayer. I had a long dream involving Bertie, Kitty, Kathleen Dunne, Barney and all of this Downey family including Úna. For me it centred around the fact that Gerry and I were divorced and that Kitty was being so understanding and even appreciative. In the dream it seemed that Kathleen either was agreeing with Kitty or something had happened in her life. And there was I innocently bicycling from Derry to Belfast through Hillhead and Maghera, no idea why, when in Maghera we were all in Úna's car [including Clare who was looking for someone in Maghera to fix her boat].

02-03-10 & 03-03-10

The favourite form of transport is motorbike, with horns blaring; government schools taught Innglish, in Islamic schools, the teaching is Hausa. Covered space, roofed space is highly valued. In the Women Farmers Advancement it was a corridor with long table, chairs round the table and screen at the top; and in at least two other meeting houses, the equivalent of a garage was the main/only meeting in essence. We visited five projects and one community which was in an extremely poor area inside the walled city

There is a working syllogism; the group experience is the premise sometimes called peer learning, but always the 'action' part is communication, by peers, radio or other interaction. If anything would not be successful then the assumption is that the communication is at fault – the result is called self-reliance [even though the result is further dependence on the group and the communication]. While accepting that this syllogism might, just might, work to bring about an economic or a feel-good change, I really must question this with the group.

Everyone is doing good work and at times even influencing policy. But there are a few concerns that almost none of the projects are becoming state funded, there is a big reliance on overseas money and very little on government or government-related funders. I observe that we are starting to become one group of Active Citizens, whereas when we started we were definitely two.

I will write about the visit to the King and Government House, and the socialising via the horses later.

Scruffy the foster dog

Twenty days short of his fifteenth birthday Scruffy is very sick. Literally on his last legs, it seems, as the back legs have a tendency to collapse under him. The dog is doing a 'Mary Clinton' who for the six weeks before she died didn't permit a drop of water or a crumb of food to cross her lips, (well I have a notion the old dog might be taking a wee sip of water in the back yard, out of sight of us humans). But let the record state, he has refused the best of his favourite pâté and any water we have tried to persuade him to lick.

Last night, at Garbhán's insistence, I lit the fire to make him more comfortable and came down at three in the middle of the night to check on him to discover when no one is looking he can get up on the big armchair all by himself. So, this wonderful dog, who was fostered out to me at six months and has now for the last fourteen-plus years lived with me, is currently being nursed by me (and I am no nurse) while family, friends and neighbours are in one mind that he deserves a few days to see if 'there's life in the old dog yet'.

The preparations for the season of goodwill have been put aside yet again – for the last eighteen years Rónán's death and anniversary account for the lack of preparation – and this year it's because of a dog... move over Rónán.

The fact that the animal is so big and heavy, coupled with Garbhán's aversion to bring any animal to the vet [in case that trip might be one-way] leads me to think that a vet house call may be required. This getting old is no joke AND costs a fortune. It is just possible the Derry taxi driver might cooperate to lift the dog when G is not looking. However, to make a liar out of me Scruffy has just now managed, reluctantly, to eat some home-cooked ham and came quickly back for more. Part of me is going "Yippee!" And the part of me that was anticipating doggie-worry-free visits to Dublin, Killough and even Manchester is now thinking those plans may have to be put on hold.

Fiachra is very fond of the dog and while slowish to contact usually, he has phoned me several times about Scruffy. I phone him back and hold the phone to Scruffy's ear… so I had better tell him about him eating the ham. I hope 'ones' will not expect me to cook specially for the animal. I think it's Emer and Paul's [niece and husband] dogs that are spoilt with the home-cooked ham.

I wouldn't mind quite so much only I had started to take Scruffy out for the late-afternoon walk to the park and was back meeting the dog owners while the dogs sniffed each other in the impolite way dogs do.

Anyhow, here I am awaiting R's Anniversary, holding a phone to a dog's ear with everyone telling me how to look after this sick hound who is loving all the attention and looking incredibly pathetic….nice act if you can get away with it.

So, Brigdín and Diarmaid will need to hold me to the promise that never ever again will I be a dog carer.

I made that very resolution after Schwartz died at nineteen – but then, when Úna and the Derry family got Scruffy (born in the Donegal townland where the monks composed the Latin-Irish hymn Deus Meus), and I seemed to be the main person on the dog-walking committee, coupled with the fact that I let him into my house whereas they kept him outside, it was inevitable that I would become hooked.

No more getting hooked.

[Editors' note: After Áine died, a very much-rallied Scruffy returned to live with Úna and Garbhán, fifteen years on, where in a seismic change of policy he was allowed inside the house.]

Schwarz the bride whisperer

Christmas Eve 2019, and Scruffy has made it to fifteen, and here am I wondering about the two influential dogs in the lives of Garbhán, Rónán, Cormac and the children who 'hung around' the Northland Road from Clarendon Street to Crawford Square during the times known as the Troubles.

Yes, Glicín MacGabhann and Schwarz Downey certainly put manners on them. Glicín, a rust wire haired potential terrier, kept the extremely beautiful MacGabhann daughters safe from the awkward advances of the young males during their gulpin stage of development; the protector of the young females was responsible for manys the broken heart.

Schwarz, called after the music teacher, Miss Schwarz, in My Dear Palestrina, was not in fact black but rather pure mongrel – the definitive multibreed – and was the comforter and protector of the boys and young men. He particularly despised people who carried plastic bags, chased them unceremoniously from the street, as poor Aodh Mag Eoin learned to his cost as he tried to sneak, on tiptoes, past the house on his way to train the City of Derry swimmers in the morning carrying his swim gear in a plastic bag. I'll say this for Hughie, he did a mean sprint.

For some unknown reason he hated motorbikes, he could hear the engine coming from miles away and the excitement reached fever pitch as any driver tried to pass the Square.

He was arrested only the once; the knock at the door and two policemen standing there one clutching Schwarz by the collar. 'Is this your dog, Missus?' And Cormac's wee friend Thomas Magee, age seven, crying real tears burbling, 'He wasn't biting me, he was stopping me running onto the road.' He wasn't even cautioned.

He was better known at the local fire station, once when he got his head stuck in the door of the wooden toy train station and a second memorable occasion when car seat belts became compulsory and he managed to lock someone in permanently, the firemen loved him for his unusual escapades!

However Schwarz's main claim to fame was as the matchmaker. A fussy eater, only the best was good enough for this mongrel rescued from the animal shelter by Rónán with his Palestrina acting money. When Garbhán brought a box of fresh cream chocolate éclairs, he had to have his share too – but the rest of us wouldn't have to go without, so long as he could drool, whine gently and make soft pleading eyes at the saft eldest son. Generally, though, he was a thoroughbred carnivore; no vegetable would touch his lips. Meaty dogfood, yes, but preferably the steak off your plate.

And so the day came when Úna was coming, off the Monaghan bus, to meet the family. I made nice wee neat salad sandwiches, even cut them into triangles, for the supper. I did not know that Úna was afraid of dogs and it was apparent that Schwarz's instincts were on red alert, when he placed the chin lovingly on her knee.

Úna then held out a salad sandwich and the flesh-eating dog ate it very politely and with apparent great relish. He didn't drool or slobber, or spit it out, and then we knew Garbhán had met 'the one'; the seal of approval had been given by Schwarz.

(When at the age of nineteen it was time for him to go, the Belfast family came to say their goodbyes on the Sunday, on the Monday Garbhán fed him a bar of chocolate, and Rónán and I brought him to the vet.)

Grá

In conversation

Áine was a friend, supporter and patron of the Your Derry group, whose mission is to improve northwest Ireland and help people to connect and collaborate. In February 2018, her friend Nicola Duffy conducted this interview with Áine for the Your Derry Facebook page.

Today I would like you to have a read of my recent chats with Dr Aine Downey
Simply – She Wins At Life.

Background and how I came to live in Derry.
Áine Máire Morton was born in Fintown on 21/09/1942 – a Christmas present conception. At two days of age my mother sent me with the godparents to the chapel, name carefully written, for the baptism and they returned to her a wee Catholic called Annie Mary – I was too young to fight the church. The train driver, a kindly man I have been told, was familiar with the task of delivering the newborns' names to the Registrar's Office, alas he had been in post many, many, years and did not approve of Irish language names, so the state in its wisdom welcomed Ethna Marie to The World.

As an adult I choose to keep both names as a reminder of the power of the Church and State and so the seeds of passionate observational and action at this early age were planted and gave life a direction (now called 'direction of travel').

I was marrying Gerry, a Derry man and, after graduating, I met with Bishop Farren and came to teach here, as simple as that.

What do I like about Derry?

Derrywoman is magnificent!

The big like is the Derry in in the margin, the margin of Ireland, the margin of the UK, the margin of Europe. Remember getting out the jotter and on the right-hand side ruling the margin; all that "rough work" and the wee right answer being stuck in the clean middle of the page? Well the realisation that the most creative work is done in the margin…that's Derry, the Ráth Mór Centre, the Pink Ladies, the playgroups, the Foyle Hospice, Northlands, An Chultúrlann, the Nerve Centre, etc. that's what I love, the creativity of this margin.

What do I not like about Derry?

Frustrations!! Begrudgery

The way you/we do not appreciate the awesome local people. When, oh when, will we get round to celebrating e.g. Conal McFeely, Brooke Park Dalton, John/Johnny McDaid, Dolores McGuinness (Lifestart), Colm Cavanagh, all the wonderful crafter – this appreciation is sorely needed and leads into what I love – how on earth did Derrywoman keep this city together through everything??? Thanks to Derrywoman, children attended the school, participated in the Féisanna, organised the baptisms, weddings, wakes, and funerals – and took the back seat!

Thanks to the tenacity and strength of Derrywoman, we have the best education for the young. But this has not been acknowledged, the creative way in which these women kept this city alive for the thirty-plus years and continue to do so. Think the Factory Girls statue and compare to the BSR monument, (buíochas, Conal).

What next???

Please put Derrywoman in charge of getting the best university courses into this city, I am tired hearing we need third-level education.

Please can we just do it!!!!!!! Open up our minds and start the creative process of the margin, a wee right answer in the middle of the page is simply not good enough.

EDUCATION CITY needs the best degrees the world has to offer, Derrywoman needs the best medical degree, the best engineering degree to make world class musical instruments, design and technology degrees by world-class universities.

And see Derrywoman, she has the sons and daughters connected with these world class Colleges and will deliver the goods.

Grá agus gach beannacht

Some Final Poems

The Opening of the Walls

I live this adult life
in the walled
Maiden City

Historical brick walls
physically barricading
questioning tradition

Prejudicial brick walls
preventing seeing
within or beyond.

[*Derry's 400-year-old city walls, which are today a
hugely popular tourist attraction, remained closed off
through much of the Troubles only re-opening in the
mid-1990s. This undated poem was written before
the Peace Process.]

Grace Before a Discussion on Feminism

I

I didn't choose to come upon you, feminism.
you came up on me
and made re-think life's experiences.
in the re-think I came to know
the spirit of my female soul,
and I apologised to her for not knowing her.

I didn't need to come upon you, feminism.
you hammered at me
through thick dense walls of believe in elitism.
I had held these values tight and dear
not counting the cost to me, female soul.
and I apologised to her for not loving her.

I didn't want to come upon you, feminism.
you snuck up on me
when I needed to believe my female worth.
My back to the ropes, holding on like grim death,
I was forced to face my female soul
and I apologised to her for abusing her.

II

Illusion it was that died
and with it package deals
of happy ever after
basking in another's soul.

Dear God, this soul
was starved of reality
the soil for our humanity

III

A whole new world to encounter
all these women-people
whose awesome spirits
only now had I the eyes to see.

IV

Waterloo Place, Derry

Deane's
"unemployment in their bones"
contrasts
with arms weighed down
by Wellworths plastic bags
cutting the palms of
deep-lined female hurting hands.
The guilt
of sometime paid employment
cultivating
face saving male bolstering
lest the walls
come tumbling down.

Máire Róisín

I hate it when you cry
it's not just
you're fighting dirty
or that
I know I've lost
it's more
you're beautiful after tears
and I am not

(Nov '92)

[*Máire Róisín, the family artist, was fourth in the 'steps of stairs'. After emigrating to London with her husband Cormac McKeever, she worked as a buyer for Harrods. She suffered a serious stroke shortly after retiring in the early 1990s. She partially recovered but relapsed a few years later, eventually succumbing in 1998, aged just 59.]

Australia with Cormac and Tracey

Travelling by train from Sydney to and through the
    Blue Mountains
Infancy and adulthood merged with the Donegal
    Blue Stack Mountains where I was born.
The climbing diesel engine, the familiar childhood
    chugging
The train driver bringing evidence of my existence to
    Ballybofey
Letting the world know that I had arrived.
In a cottage up in the Blue Mountains, I watch as a
    totally citified son
Takes great pride in lighting the modern wood-
    burning stove
And I am thinking of my mother needing the fire
To heat the old house, to cook the food and warm
    the water
And the damp Blue Stack mountainy turf.
Outdoors the smell of the wood burning is as seductive
As that first whiff of the turf smoke when you cross
    into Donegal
Indoors I stir my tea with a little commemorative
    spoon
And I remember Auntie Florrie and the Apostle
    spoons for the soft-boiled eggs.
The first wearing of my rainbow socks to walk the
    cliff-edge path
Around Grose Valley
From Govetts Leap to Pulpit Rock

In the eucalyptus-blue mountains
The first Sunday after the first Easter
Of a son now living in the other world.

Was the god Thor tempted by our orange plastic
    emergency ponchos
Or by the Grand Canyon potential to echo and
    reverberate?
And Thor did not come alone
Sheet lightning and big fat splats of rain
    accompanied him to add to the adventure
Being from Derry,
Thor's powers over us were limited by Colmcille
Many hundred years ago
But you had to be impressed by the rumble echo
Around and around the molecules of white mist
Resting on the eucalyptus trees
Covering the valley.
The laughter when not one of us
Fell into the flooded brook
With the fair weather stepping stones.

The mountains connect
With an excited full-of-party news
Family at home
And the mountain dreaming connected with
A slightly dismissive
'I'm only dead', smiling son
And it felt right and proper that in this vast
Blue mountainy place

The past and present could come together
To protect,
Bless
And safeguard
The way forward
For all of us.

In the Blue Mountains
I left behind the orange plastic ponchos
And a wee bit of my soul;
And I brought with me,
The memories of the laughter,
The exuberance,
The Thor accompaniment
And our spiritual connectedness

And two pebbles from Pulpit Rock for Rónán's grave.

Le grá

From A Hotel Window

Young woman in a red skirt
crisp white short-sleeved blouse
bare legs, slightly tanned
designer lunchbox
in her left hand
Those women's magazine stories
of park bench accidental meetings
on warm sunshine days
inevitably leading to the…
makes going to work
on a June Monday morning
full of anticipatory pleasure
and puts a spring in her step.

The professional Asian woman
middle management at least
quality-cultivated traditional dress
brief case in her left hand
bulging Sainsbury's plastic bag
in her right
The house cleaned and now
the evening meal in hand
Can give concentrated attention
to demonstrate being equal to the man
She gives the brief case a wee swing
and hurries on her way.

Adolescent woman-girl
she does not want to be
refuses to acknowledge the sunshine
Heavy black leggings, DM's on feet
school uniform covered by
heavyweight dirty dull jacket
the laden book bag
over slumped shoulders
nothing is going to bring pleasure
to her this day
Full of the burden of emerging womanhood
she drags her feet to
wherever, whatever.

And the men drive by
in their cars.

By Candlelight

January 2002

Early evening
Three candles lit
Sitting at the kitchen table
Listening to Edith Piaf
Using the 'waiting for the family' time
As the excuse
For seeming to do nothing.

Helen Waddell was right
'You see more by candle light'
An island of light
Focuses the page
The candle shadows
Bring their own brand of flickering
I move one candle so that
The line of the pencil
And the shadow of the pencil
Are as one.
The two cats, narrow-eyed,
Monitor the hand pencil movement
And prepare to pounce.

The glow of the candles
Shows me the limits of the 'now'
– as far as the candles illuminate
And I wonder which of the

Intricate illustrations of the
Book of Kells came into life in this light
And which harmonies of 'Deus Meus Adiuva Me'
Beckoned chanting into the candlelight.

The blessed candles of the night
Each burns so differently.
I should remember the gases
From Bunsen burner days
And smile at how much
I have forgotten.
Once upon a time
Not being able to name and draw in position
The coal mines of South Wales
Would have failed geography,
Transient information, reproduced to gain certificates,
Coal fields gone, certificates lost
Yet I remember all my teachers
And whisper roll call their presence.

So what is important candlelight?
Candle – kindly light – right enough.
You hear better in this light,
I am so pleased that I was reintroduced to Edith Piaf.
 The perfect music for candlelight,
Her heady humming
And everything stops for "L'amour"
The vitality, life for the living
The pain, the joy, the hollering
 The loving

Of whatever it is I am doing now
Giving the now my all.

The blatant, busy nowness of Christmas
The New Year and 'Nollaig na mBán', The Women's
Christmas,
No longer the now
It almost feels self-indulgent to rest
And the candlelight of understanding tells me
Between that human milestone and the next
Needs come the fallow time
Acknowledging the nurturance
Given out
To listen
Hear, absorb
Soul's journey
A time
For giving in.

In grief

In October 2006, on the way home from saying 'Grá, a rún' to Cormac in Manchester, I called into the Liverpool John Lennon Airport Chaplaincy, and the seeds for this train of thought were planted.

I am finding that it is in leaving Cormac in Australia, Manchester, New Zealand – wherever – that this leaving a living son identifies wee corners of the departure of Rónán to the other world.

As you walk with grief
Walk slowly, pausing often
Do not hurry
It does not help the journey

When memories come unbidden
Bringing that intense emotion
Cherish the discovery
That death cannot take memory away

Be gentle with the soul
Who walks with grief
And if it is yourself,
Be gentle with yourself.

Until the time when you
Can live with their life
And not with their departure
Take time, be gentle.

From 'Conversations With God'

If you knew who you are –
that you are the most magnificent,
the most remarkable,
the most spending being God has ever created –
you would never fear

But you do not know who you are
and you think you are a great deal less.

Grá

[*This poem appears to be the only surviving relic of
a larger collection.}

The Soul Of A Book

Oh I did work hard
I tried and tried
to believe the book that said
'with practice it's as simple
as pencil on paper'.
Yes, it may well be
the process is simple
BUT
it takes an awful
lot of words to fill
a word processor page
and I don't have those
many words on anything
And then I wonder what happens the words
that always disappear
between putting in and printing out
where do they go?
This room is filled with flying words
like in limbo
going round and round.
Little wonder the window blind
simply collapsed tonight,
the weight of those lost words
AND
You can't curl up
in front of the fire
glass on hearth
with a word processor.

Listening to the flames
feeling the heat on
cheeks, forehead
the brightness lighting
and shadowing the page,
hand automatically strolling
with thoughts, feelings.
The soul in hand.

Meditation

Cover me with soft earth,
and with every shovelful
throw in a handful of lily, jasmine
and wild rose seeds,
that they might grow over my grave
diffusing in the air
the fragrance of my heart
and as they blow with the breeze
may they remind passers-by
of my dreams and aspirations.

Return to your homes
and you will discover there
what death cannot steal
from me or from you.

Grá
Áine

Do Áine chaoin chróga
In Memoriam

An tÉan Beag

Sciurd sé isteach
sa tseomra samhraidh
Satharn na stoirme
mhúch mé an míshuaimneas
ionam a d'éirigh
comhartha báis a leithéid
i measc mo mhuintire

Bheannaigh mé dó
ag guí go n-imeodh sé
an doras amach

Trí lá dár gcionn
tháinig an droch scéal
fógra do bháis
tú faoi shuaimhneas.

Bhí leath-chois agat
ar an taobh eile
de shíor
i dteagmháil
le do mhuintir
oilithrí
ar shlí na fírinne

romhat
á seoladh
chun na beatha sioraí.

Fionnuala Geary, May 2020

For brave and gentle Áine
In Memoriam

The Little Bird

He skirted inward
into the summer room
the Saturday of the storm
I settled the unrest in me
that such an omen of death
can rise
among my kin

I blessed him
praying he would go out
the open door

Three days later
the bad news came,
the word of your death,
and that you were at rest.

You always had half-a-foot
on the other side
already
in touch with
your pilgrim
people
who sailed out

before you
on the true passage
to everlasting life.

Fionnuala Geary, May 2020